DANIEL GABRIEL

COLUMBUS

GNOSIS PRESS
NEW YORK

The Gnosis Press Edition

The editors gratefully acknowledge the assistance of the New York City Department of Cultural Affairs Materials for the Arts Program.

Cover design by Henry Iva

Published by Gnosis Press
Gnosis Press
P.O. Box 42
Prince Street Station
New York, N.Y. 10012
USA

Library of Congress Cataloging-in-Publication Data

Gabriel, Daniel. 1946-
     Columbus / Daniel Gabriel. — 1st ed.
     p. cm.
     ISBN 0-922792-55-0 : $12.00

1. Columbus, Christopher—Poetry.   2. America—Discovery and exploration—Poetry. 3. Explorers—Poetry. I. Title.
PS3557. A24C64 1993
811' .54—dc20   92-38307
                                                          CIP

Printed in the United States of America

For Marlen and my mother

ACKNOWLEDGMENTS AND NOTE

The following poems of the Prologue (some in different form) originally appeared in the journal *Gnosis*, to which grateful acknowledgment is made: "Embarking," "Rondure," "The Mysterium," "At the Level of the Signifier I," "At the Level of the Signifier II," "Star I," "Star II," "Star III," "The Hollow Text of Night," "Cormorant I," and "Cormorant II."

I would also like to record my thanks to, among others, Daniel P. Quinn, Artistic Director of The New Stagecraft Company, Inc., for supporting this work from its inception through a series of readings; and my wife, Marlen, for listening to and critically reading the work at various stages of its development.

The world of this work is mostly fictional, but the historical record concerning Columbus and the Columbian and pre-Columbian epochs has been freely drawn upon, particularly for aspects of Book One and significant aspects of Books Two through Five. (The Prologue, Books Six and Seven, and the Epilogue should be read as largely constructions of the imagination.) It goes without saying that a number of textual, as well as nontextual, "sources" have been instrumental in the composition of this work, but for the historical record I am most indebted to the following authors: Hans Koning, Samuel Eliot Morison, Marco Polo, Kirkpatrick Sale, and Christopher Columbus himself.

CONTENTS

PROLOGUE   13

Embarking   15

Solitude   17

Soarer of Seas   18

Rondure   19

Dream of Maria's Grief   20

Doubt and Redemption   21

Blue Death   22

Storm and Stress   23

The Galactic Lash   24

The Mysterium   25

At the Level of the Signifier I   26

At the Level of the Signifier II   27

The Oscillation   29

The Presence of the Present   30

In the Sky the Image of Calm   31

Sun   32

The Plain of Reverie   33

Thick Time   34

Dark Vowels   35

Star I   36

Star II   37

Star III   38

The Door, The Sea   39

White Veil   40

A Conversation With Divinity   42

The Hollow Text of Night   44

Simulacrum   46

Fever I   48

Fever II   50

Cormorant I   52

Cormorant II   54

The Paradigm of Formal Space   55

Moon I   57

Moon II   59

Breathing the World   61

BOOK ONE: EARLY LIFE   63

I. Hymn to the Atlantic   65

II. Passage of the Heart   67

  The Family   67

  Dwelling   69

  Repast   71

  Room of the Sea   72

  Infancy and Memory   74

  Ambition I   76

  Seeing Maria   78

  Ambition II   80

III. Ode to Memory   82

IV. Imago Mundi   84

  The Word   84

  Destiny   86

  Ambition III   88

  A History of My Life at Sea   90

  Sources of Light   94

  At the Court of Isabella   96

V. Maria's First Monologue   98

BOOK TWO: THE FIRST VOYAGE   101

I. Hymn to Cathay   103

II. Voyage of Discovery   105

   Ships of State   105

   The Expulsion of the Jews   107

   Itinerary of Fear   109

   Letter to Maria   111

   The Mind's Mutiny   113

   Between Desire and Landfall   115

III. Ode to History   117

IV. The Other   119

   Bridging   119

   Admiration of the Visible   121

   Terra Firma   123

   The Death of the Santa Maria   125

   Tempest and Winter's World   126

   Restless Triumph   128

V. Maria's Second Monologue   129

BOOK THREE: THE SECOND VOYAGE   133

I. Hymn to Hispaniola   135

II. Imperial Dream   137

  Stately Power   137

  The Problematics of Experience   139

  Passage to Paradise   141

  The Canoe   142

  Reprisal in Hispaniola   144

III. Ode to Power   146

IV. Imperial Conquest   148

  A Vision   148

  A Theory of the State   150

  The Ethics of Slavery   152

  Primal Gold   154

  The Earth of Christendom   156

  Return and Review   157

V. Maria's Third Monologue   159

BOOK FOUR: THE THIRD VOYAGE 161

I. Hymn to the Indies 163

II. To the Shores of Paradise 165

 At the Altar of Another Voyage 165

 To Act Without Signs 167

 Unlock the Sign 169

III. Ode to Invention 171

IV. The Earth Closed Off 173

 On the Nature of Rebellion 173

 Chains and Metaphysics 175

V. Maria's Fourth Monologue 178

BOOK FIVE: THE FOURTH VOYAGE 181

I. Hymn to the Terrestrial Paradise 183

II. Trials and Persecutions 186

 The Sea as Origin 186

 Repulsed 188

 Veragua and Destiny 190

III. Ode to Perseverance   192

IV. Marooned   195

    To the Face of God   195

    The Python   198

V. Maria's Fifth Monologue   201

BOOK SIX: RETIREMENT I   205

I. Hymn to An Other World   207

II. The Seven Deadly Sins, Part I   209

    Prelude   209

    Pride   211

    Wrath   213

    Sloth   215

    Envy   217

III. Ode to Humility   220

IV. The Seven Deadly Sins, Part II   222

    Avarice   222

    Gluttony   224

Lechery   226

Coda: The Python II   228

V. Maria's Sixth Monologue   230

BOOK SEVEN: RETIREMENT II   233

I. Hymn to Oceania   235

II. Meditations, Part I   237

  Farewell to God   237

  Ars Poetica I   240

  Ars Poetica II   243

  Ars Poetica III   244

III. Ode to Prophecy   246

IV. Meditations, Part II   248

  Lunar Sun/Solar Moon   248

  The Austere Light of Possibility   250

V. Maria's Seventh Monologue   252

EPILOGUE   255

The Transcendence of Apollo   257

PROLOGUE

(AT SEA, ON THE FIRST VOYAGE)

EMBARKING

weighed by sea, not a way
but the way, the only giant
in storm, fish and flesh,
tossed and crushed, the seas
in my thoughts the waves

in my hands, this way
that I go.
I will go, giant in my
cabin, monster of the
visitations, send me onward

into the horizon's gleam
glimmer of ascent
astute sailor, buoyant spirit,
I need go.
I who had laughed in Madrid

at the fool's costume
laugh now at the wrench
of the ship, wretched crew
in their tears, their hands
braced red, they need go,

forgetting exhaustion.
the sea has never melody,
but a chorus of hell
high-strung and clever,
singing ironies from

scorched tongues. they
and the giant of heaven's
choir syncopate.
I meditate in the realm
of my act, my act among

these chains of waves.
I create the sea for the
moment, but remembering
God I reject the moment
and kiss the other,

that wind in his cheeks.
sucking now and blowing . . .
the sea becomes his sky
in its steel heat.
(I will never forget you.)

my mind now blank
in the room of roiling furniture
and sacred charts.
I who had laughed in Madrid
at the fool's costume,

laugh now at my dread.
thunder of my heart
soul-beats of waves!
crew's drenched hair
lapping the white seed!

SOLITUDE

O sea, enchanting lady
or miserable man
without manners, carrying
us aloft, afloat in the
middle of the world

(my crew asleep with
the wind nestled
in their ears). O sea, bring us
to Cathay, exotic home
of merchants and wizards,

of ancient texts whose
language unfastens
the knot of the
universe: that enigma
of my soul.

paradise, O paradise . . .
God, I look upon your
Creation with innocent
eyes, and my Maria looks too
across the vertiginous space.

(I shall never forget you.)
this paradise of mind
imagining the mind
of paradise, God and the
inner depths (enchanting lady)—

frothy and splayed wide
the planet of our synthetic
constructions and the pure
bliss of memory (Maria,
wait for me).

SOARER OF SEAS

I seek for words
to tell my thoughts,
but they elude me; my
love is too abstract and
radiant. her hair, so bright,

flew up and dark,
like sails at seashore.
I have her image now
without the words. memory
has never been so good to me—

forward-moving always, trained
to leap time like waves.
waves untamed, no language in
the fixed and tussled sea.
why words,

when her hair turns
darkness into sun,
when her beauty stabs me
in the brain?
because words speak memory,

because they stop
the torture. yet memory
troubles me when visions
rise to conquer mystic
borders. to stay awake—

the wave, the future,
quantum physics, macrouniverse.
(Columbus—to see,
to conquer. Columbus,
soarer of seas.)

RONDURE

O sea, O stars, the curves
of three dimensions: we have
no land as rounded as the sun.
the man in the moon winks
at the rondure of the approaching

ship. O Cathay, spinning
wearily ahead but in some
distant prehistoric space:
the locus of three dimensions—
the calculus of gold.

so I had seen it, in the room
of the three spheres, rich with
yellow filaments and minerals—
the cadavers awaking by the
shining foliage of the man-made.

O sea, O stars, O God,
God before the abstract
spirit descended into the
portals, and vestibules,
into the lexicon of prayer.

behold the gold made
holy by the light of him,
naked before the angels.
he speaks the raw speech
of alchemy in the third

dimension. I will dare
to see through this veil
the perfect movement
of the solar system: the god
of latent destiny.

DREAM OF MARIA'S GRIEF

sleep inside, the tides' throat quiet.
(Columbus, gatherer of waves.)
the dream of destiny
made splendid by the
muted pontification

of this night. the dream
arrives in measures:
it is Maria crying by
the dying body of her
mother: the broken nuptial

of the form in a room
fractured by the image
dissolving and revolving—
Maria undone and about to
wreck her sacraments.

(beauty never found my wife.
she discovered it in the
humblest of places: inside
my hands one day. she
realized the map could lead

to Cathay.) . . . the dream
exploded into a thousand
shards of crystal; the form
careened off eternity.
Maria observed the apocalypse.

her mother was left empty
but not without the memory of
sweet-chanting time; it was
Maria's body as vessel now bearing
her dead mother into the image of eternity.

DOUBT AND REDEMPTION

solitude, and the disquieting
thought that it may all come
to nothing; yet the albatross
this morning was prophetic.
of what?

the sea is turbulent tonight.
my dream awakes me.
what can we make of the narrative
of sleep? sailing into oblivion
we hope for miracles, a vision

of the muscular oarsman
who rows from morning till night,
or of the woman who turns
our fears into her dark.
the sea needs no company.

why do I tremble so?
why do I sweat with anxiety
despite the great project ahead?
what makes me shake
as if I am about to die?

it is all night
and it is all distance
and the sea will swallow us
if we let it.
let there be magic,

let there be image-production.
I swallow the air
of the sea-foul wind
and my eyes see clear
my eyes . . . see clear.

BLUE DEATH

metaphysical sea,
physical force,
blue death.
shape of the consciousness,
form of the unconscious—

on this new day, I query
your motives. are you the
charming suitor who woos
his mistress
with an empty sublime?

or the brazen woman
whose dream
of equanimity assures
a healing of all wounds
between the sexes?

on what can we count:
metaphysics or the theorems
of mathematicians?
is it fate or fact
with which we must contend?

I put you out there,
and yet force of my storm
form of my waves
delirious and calm sea,
you weigh in the oceanic heart.

STORM AND STRESS

once, in a dark minute of
my youth, I was pursued
by waves. crashing against
my fists, breaking into
my lungs, lashing at my ankles,

they stood and rolled,
rolled and stood.
next to death, I was drenched
from my mind to the notion
of space, my best suit of clothes

ringing with salt, and fishes
flapping; my ears clapped shut.
who invented God?
what magisterial race,
what fearless genius—

and would he ever let me be?
I was never young in his eyes.
marked, I questioned the sky
and it too seemed to pursue me
with waves of rain

and eagles of hail
and bolts of angels
stabbing into the child
I imagined I could one day be.
his wrath had spoken.

THE GALACTIC LASH

why daydream about the future
when the present stares
back at me with turbulent eyes?
searching for one's destiny
makes no sense

when the sea climbs
the portholes, or the sharks
plying the waves hunger
for the man-meat.
I can write epitaphs

for the past, yet there
in front of me the waves
roar for my life, and the
ship's too, bounty
of the world.

visions of paradisal
beaches and globular fruit,
tropical enchantments,
or the East and gold,
scope down in the serpent's

galactic lash.
mind makes no difference
in the matter of the sea.
I had better live this drama
of our holocaust.

THE MYSTERIUM

inside the sea,
awakes an ancient history:
fossil texts
of the wordless encounters
between life and the superbeing.

take us back even as
the sea rolls angrily,
even as the eyes press forward
upon the Orient *mysterium*.
beauty of chaos arranging

itself into crystal order;
beauty of the white magic:
the texts speak their secrets
of the turbulent struggle
for equilibrium.

inside memory, slumber
of the sea unfolding.
take me back to her arms
whose embrace
enchains freedom.

harmony of the deep past
dark rhythms of the text
whose music's prayer recites
the code upon which I wait.
it is all the other

and the me enfolded in
her arms. if the memory fails,
will this ancient history
unfurl its text beyond
the other-me?

AT THE LEVEL OF THE SIGNIFIER I

the sea is my signifier,
for him beyond human discourse.
I stand humble before his
Creation; yet language creates
something of his intended fiction.

or is it fiction that I see
with my full mind the outward-
bound waves, and the gulls
swimming before the rim of
the sun? is it fiction that

the sharks play havoc
at my very feet? he has
created time in his own image,
yet I count its measures
across the breadth of the

illimitable space.
my sea is signifier,
the sequence of disorder I
give to order and the reverse.
his magic of the real is my fiction.

let us speak together:
he in his monologism,
I in my dispersed syntax,
plurality of words and waves,
men beaten to their global difference.

AT THE LEVEL OF THE SIGNIFIER II

I mean to say,
in the year of our Lord 1492,
that at times I speak in
paradoxes; or that time
framed by a date

is deceptive. his World
is Real, as real as the
storm that rose up following
last night's prayer,
crashing against our sea-house,

our water-ground, as if
he hoped to put Being out
of existence, and our project
into the useless text of
a disavowal.

I can never approach
his real through my language.
yet my language approaches
his real through its
own inimitable

devices, and without it
he could not exist . . .
torture of sentences and words,
will he beat me?
cursed breath,

slime of my blood,
I have let the syntax
of my air disturb the
harmony. carry us, sea, into
a language of redemption.

transport us beyond the
final stage of the dialectic
when his mouth utters
the monologic wound, the
shattering of all texts

of truce. at the level of
the signifier, I hold my
world up by the delicate web
of a noun, but his real
speaks in silent apocalypse.

THE OSCILLATION

between the trauma and
quiescence—he forgave—
is the void we cannot avoid.
the oscillation of light
and dark at the center

of the brain. the ephemeral
flash, repeating at intervals:
will I live, will I die?
the sea sits in peace,
tidy in its unruly majesty.

I wait for another flash.
the ship, my lucky home
beneath me, tugs me out of
this insatiable repetition:
will I live, will I die?

the crew, too, dismal
in their dreams, coerce
another tension: the lucky
question of survival in
the thunderclaps of his world.

will I live, will I die?
and then the sea in its
miracle of blue brine,
its textured light, opens
in a calm, somnambulant vortex;

and it's gone—as sudden as
its power overcomes the day
and all the urge of life,
sunk beneath the reverie
of God's sea.

THE PRESENCE OF THE PRESENT

wrapped in his grace
smooth sailing for two days
not even tempestuous thoughts
to wrack my body:
free, breathe out

swimming into space.
the sun settles over starboard.
venture now, the paradigm
of possibility: O longings
for the *mysterium*.

but no; stay; quiet; calm;
quiet stay. listen to the
beat of the heart or the pulse
in the hand held splayed.
watch the sun as if

it rested for the last time . . .
when was it I rested?—
stay; quiet; calm—
never still, to be regenerated
in the moment,

to be born anew as each
instant passes, undisturbed
by my "I." stay; quiet;
calm; and the sun preaches
a lesson of the good.

IN THE SKY THE IMAGE OF CALM

in this exploration, with the sea
beneath us speaking its mind:
waves ascending against us,
water in its long ennui
disturbing the quiet of

visions, shutting down all
dream of conquest. this sea
beneath us unloosing its seed
of violence, grey floods,
white pinnacles . . .

a traumatic spell.
in this exploration, the sea
drives our sight and consciousness
(the text upon which we frame
our discourse).

but the sky sits in passive
radiance, awaiting the
message of the superbeing.
I look to it for peace
from the sea's grip

and grimace, from
my own drive and despair.
O sky, what lesson do you
hold for us who seek
the invisible *mysterium* beyond?

SUN

featureless sun, steady and
penetrating, fixed form
in a sky whose very form
is change. I stand at the bow
today wishing for rain.

my eyes see myriad shapes,
apparitions in the air, or
dance-phantoms upon the
white sea. I spin in place—
no hope for rain in this sun.

who walks there? over
my shoulder I see Maria
pacing the deck. she wears white
to mourn the absence of her husband.
there are no letters of our love

across the ocean space.
what next, she asks?
will our love drown in the
depths of sea and sky?
will you bequeath only a memory?

my death means nothing now.
my only vision a sun that cares
little for the aspiration
of its fire. what do I hear?
some music from the sea,

a vexing noise, my mind's skitters.
I ask for cool; cold earth in
my hands; a wave on board.
but only this scorching flame.
wait for me.

THE PLAIN OF REVERIE

asleep, awake, afloat—
arisen from the dead. God,
redeem this adventure from
the sloth of sea and mind.
despite my earlier

transgression, I remain . . .
sanctify this quest.
love alone and the vision
of the *mysterium* cannot
undo the apocalypse.

adventure of the moon
on high seas, sharks gnawing
at the water—smelling
human flesh. break the trauma
of the quick leap from dull

to demonic. the dangerous
image of paradise: tropical fruit
and the fanfare of
nature's banquet;
orisons of the sea-swell between

frozen beauty and motile pain.
God, affix the wave
to the woman: *mysterium*
and the long dress across
the plain of reverie. Maria.

THICK TIME

the love of man and woman,
unuttered, cannot revive
the pleasure of first sight.
only words will dress the
white of the first faltering

embrace. experience is not
enough. we have as a man-
race enough of the storm
of space, the dripping of time
aboard this island of the world.

without words, I cannot
love you. but without love
there is no bridge to marry
water and shore.
I stand isolated now

in a crowd of restless dwellers.
yet words will leap like
swallows to your mirage
across the infinite edge
of ocean, across thick time.

wait for me, for I have
words to adorn your
soul-name, to make
of marriage a valence of
two elements of the beyond.

DARK VOWELS

this way that we go
on the waste of the long
grain of sea: this waste
or the glorious blue?
I am beginning to doubt

my ability to doubt.
is it waste or the glory of God,
or does my mind wander too
far from sight?—the light
of heaven, or the

polluted doom of hell?
the end or the beginning
of majesty? the whale's plain
power, or the phantom gull?
and then I open my eyes

and find Maria, as brilliant
as an albatross—
silent except for her eyes,
dark vowels through
the steely sea.

STAR I

I would like to surrender
to the star, unfetter the bonds
of this earth, sing with
the heavens and spheres.
I would like to forget

and in forgetting
perhaps to remember the
magic of destiny. star,
take up this heaviness
within your humble brilliance.

make the load on my
shoulders lighter, and in
my heart uncoil this hissing
pain. link your light
to the dark sweat of my hands.

star, remember for my
memory the real, rescue
the sea-bloated spirit.
I would like to surrender
and negate the sign for the star

and then in the empty
clothes upon the deck
tie my name within the
fine thread of consciousness
and voyage into space.

STAR II

the path of the star
leads to a time before
the prophet's predictions,
before war and human
affliction, before Good

was severed from Evil.
I stand here shaken
by the winds of Hell, hoping
for that pure light again
to rock me back to innocence.

the cannonade blasts
through my heart thousands
of miles away; missiles lodge
in my skull; meteors, now
weapons, blind my sight;

the starving of peasants
penetrates my mind's walls.
I hear the individual death
through the cannonade, the last breath
frozen on the sea's casement.

I stand here shaken
by the winds of Hell, hoping
for the language of one life,
the prelapsarian purity,
the point of crystal and quintessence,

while all along the fractured vowels
rain terror upon the fleeing
planet. who can help regenerate
that purloined time before this
war consumes even our ocean-earth?

STAR III

I awake in a sweat
of disconnection: all my
body discolored; but it is
a disease of the mind:
the turbulent river of memory,

the spiraling future,
the stinging present: hand
pounding upon ship's stern.
I lose myself in a sea
of serpents: they wrap

around my dream-heart,
choke off the iridescent
hope of the *mysterium*,
strangle the voice
of empire.

I unloose my violence
upon the orderly world,
undo the knot that held
hand to star, destroy
the code of the enigma.

what will keep the dialectic
in its place, so that
once more beyond the
fractured dawn I walk
the path of the starry oracle?

THE DOOR, THE SEA

before the sea, there
was only the room,
with many paintings—
all in earth color; before
the door opened onto

the sea, there was only
the door that looked
back to the earth. I spent
years interpreting these
paintings to the thousands

who entered, I who looked
innocent enough. before
the door I waited for word
from the stormy spaces, the
thrusting sails and cutting

waves. I had hoped
for direct contact with
the superbeing, to ride
clenched to a whale.
before the door I could see

my life unfolding and
death laughing and
the thousands tearing
the sublime. I coughed
in solitude. now I can

remember that first
hallelujah of the rushing
sea, door broken
and myself lifted into
the orisons of his eyes.

WHITE VEIL

in anticipation rests desire,
in desire the anxious voice.
what leads us to infinity
leads us to our deaths.
we sail with desire

and long for the vague
paradigm of our dream.
to do otherwise
would be to sink
forever into an abyss

of the future. what validates
us is the gleam of the
unknown, the vortex
of the *mysterium*.
the superbeing seduces

from his margin of desire;
he urges failure, or
the success of catastrophe.
the ships will not plummet
from a flat earth

but from a will that flattens
in the holocaust of the
never-seen, the froth
and foam of the uncertain,
the quaking of the sea

in his hands. breath in
and out, the throat aches
with the fever of the
distant earth. O,
what do you want from us?

what can we give you
now and at the hour of
our deaths? our eyes smart
from the white light,
white veil of infinitude.

A CONVERSATION WITH DIVINITY

cast away at his door,
rejected because of my
blasphemies, I take stock
of my life in the greatness
of his project. how humble

we all are, but humbler
when his eyes look away,
when he no longer addresses us.
I am watching his lips
for recognition, but his speech

concerns the oceans and fishes,
the sea-diving cormorant,
the daystar, and the
rumbling earth of Asia.
how humble . . .

and as if I could free
myself from humility,
my mind chased his
greatness, raced against
the tides of his ascent.

thirsting for his salt,
hungering for the eel
that flutters in the sea,
I myself took on his image,
aspired to the power of his

holocaust . . . and now I
take stock: make magic
of the real, the humility
of our lingering stench.
we sea horses fish

for worms in the skeletal
bottom of the sea. no plants
but dry weeds even there.
(I recognize friends
who walked off the earth

as well, longing for
infinity.) and I turn
once again to the sky-blue
death, expecting, that is,
the worst for my continuing

transgressions, and he
answers with only the
faintest reply: take stock,
take stock, our projects
do not intersect, and

the sea ahead is beset by
maelstroms, the earth
swims into an abyss. take stock—
for you will fare better
in the greatness of humility.

and somberly crossing the
threshold into my cabin,
I notice that nothing looks
the same, nothing is as before—
all furniture upset,

all maps deracinated.
in that moment the world
was pulled apart—not destroyed,
but disturbed. and I sit in the
perfect stillness of the end.

THE HOLLOW TEXT OF NIGHT

the sea opens and I fall,
but then Maria calls,
and I sit up straight—
braced against the lumber
between myself and the world.

the world opens and I see
nothing for miles above
the horizon or below,
nothing for miles of past
and future. only a dull

present whose numbness
I cannot penetrate. is that
a sea gull in the mist,
a cooing bird, or palaver
rising from the text?

what am I reading:
life or fiction? how does
my mind work upon the
objects that seem to cross
my path? how do I sense,

or will I ever again?
my mind turns and turns,
the questions turn upon
themselves: an infinite
progression of rhetorical leaps.

what can I learn from
the hollow text of night:
sheer emptiness of perception,
sheer blankness of receding
walls? what can I learn

from the sea gull whose
eyes seem horror struck
by my mind: tabula
rasa of the death
that exceeds the dead?

SIMULACRUM

not a paradise of lemon
trees and cactus and
blue lakes, not a paradisal
pact between God and humans,
but a white beach

whose line stretches to
nothingness and a barren
text the master code
of which is monologic discourse.
I am making myself over

in the frame of a question mark
and peer out from this
blank beach into a white,
uninterrupted sky.
I am myself a margin

between earth and sea,
but an inept measure
of reality, between zero
and the far reaches of negation.
an isolated mind on

an isolated sea, an island
whose shores swell to its center,
an engine of discord.
I pace the sands searching
for some trace of memory,

of the future with its
vast spectacles, oracular
poetry, and the blue circle
of definition.
but only this, this

simulacrum rises before
me, as if on a desert and
not a seashore, a desert
where birds peck at my
brain as I observe.

FEVER I

the sun upon my head
pours like molten lead.
I repel all thought of
ambition. I am burning
alive in its rays, I am about

to utter my will to the vast
ocean of waste and ennui.
I make a confession to
my God who looks askance;
what name does he go under

now? my mind whirls
in the vicissitudes of heat
and cold: the fever of my
marginal existence. I pace
the ship in the rounds of a

sentry, but without the state
as my womb. what name
can I apply to my fever,
how can I penetrate its core?—
as if to understand it

would be to free myself
from its tentacles. but
perhaps I should enjoy
its frozen heat, the sun
pouring its molten lead

into my blood vessels,
the very presence of sensation
in this numb time.
perhaps I should surrender
to the massive force

of the furnace in my skull,
the sun deconstructing
the alphabet of my
cartography, all motion
of the ship's longing swim.

and then, happy to have
the love of death, I can
laugh at the frivolous efforts
of the muscular oarsman, whose
boat splits in a single wave.

FEVER II

how can the mind speak,
with what verbs of mourning
for the loss of time-sense?
what language to choose
within a babel of discourse?

to begin to articulate
dementia, the sleep of
the passionate quest, the
sweep of the storm across
the deck—wiping all traces

from the brain. that is
the conflict of even my
primordial roots. can
the sea give us language,
such sea that moves indifferent

to our struggles to
conquer self? can God,
whose mind knows neither
human time or space or death?
I am posing these questions

even as I forget my name.
or was it that language
came only after the fading
of the prelapsarian light,
when the senses

grew complex in the conscious
mind? I am at the border
of some discovery, but do not
have the language to uncover it.
I call on magic,

I call on the miracle of the
fishes; what hurts me so much
that I cannot even speak
of it? and to look outside
seems only infinity.

in the half-light of the
moon, I attempt a simple
act of sight—
but all goes blind
in this sleep.

CORMORANT I

today I see a cormorant
off starboard and am
jolted back into a moment
of perception—but it
swoops down for a fish

and flies off. it is
only the cormorant my
vision embraces, and
it is only a flash of light
that brings it to me,

and even then I wonder
did I see it, or was it
another delusion upon which
I constitute my life?
how long can I live

in the nether shadows
of a sleep without dream,
of a fever whose very
intensity dissolves all
sensation? I seek a

language at least of
the absence, a formal
geometry to describe
the shapelessness. perhaps
a science to register

the modulations of the void.
I call on memory, but it
resists my longings, I
call on the sea, and it
throbs in my inner ear—

but there it vanishes.
what month is it?
how many moons before
the sea will throw me back
as unworthy? or will a stream

carry us into a fractious
sky? the cormorant alights
on the bowsprit and seems
to stare into the heart of
my doubt. I call to it,

come, come, we will dance together
in the air, we will make light
of my sickness. but it wants
no part of this consumption:
air and fire, earth and sea.

CORMORANT II

the rapacious cormorant
feasts off the sea, but
I at least have this one
image. yet, would it not be
better to sleep than to be

reminded of the sheer
destruction we are all
indicted in? would it not
be better to die than to
take part in the slaughter

of his Creation, the explosion
of his text upon the sea?
I have my moment of the
cormorant and follow its
flight of destruction.

can I not at least
rechannel its drive to kill
into the azure magnitude
I force myself to resurrect,
or construct a drama

of mind upon object
to distract it from its
fated purpose? will it
destroy if I feed it bread,
will it devour if I sing

to it? and yet these are all
meditations I cannot
reason with. O fever that
longs to wrench mind from body,
O demon of apocalypse.

THE PARADIGM OF FORMAL SPACE

I attempt to separate myself
from my circumstances,
from even the lumber
that stands between myself
and the world,

to observe every minute
detail of this prison cell
of the present. I attempt
to delineate its shapes and
to comprehend all that has

led to this moment—this
moment that I cannot
articulate in any language
as simply as through forms:
circles and spheres and

rectangles of blasphemy.
but as I attain the
paradigm of formal space,
all goes wavy in the brain,
such discord I cannot

utter. I want to scream
so that the very depths will
hear me, so that the fishes
will dash from the thunderous
weight of my voice.

how have I come to this,
so that even the question
becomes difficult to formulate?
how will it end?
the lumber of the ship

rocks me into a dizzying
spin; I stand spread-eagled
over a pit, and there the
tigers of the sea mangle
my men one by one.

MOON I

it was a pale moon and deep,
and I spoke to it in a
conversation of despair.
I could see it clearly:
no night dream came

between us; not even a
night sky, but motionless
ether. my eyes filled
with this strange beauty
as if I had died—

and filled again with
a mystical life. I was
transported into an
air of syntax and
semantics blown over

by direct communion,
bright face of confession,
despair in danger of
articulation. who could say
in the drenched light

of despair, I had not
witnessed a bloody vision
of creation, the cremation
of a sperm whale come back
from death to spout

anew? or was it once again
a mirage of the many-
folded mind, one image built
upon another, so that no heart
could speak with any certainty

of the truth? moon, speak
back some light to me who
runs with neither fire nor
intention: spindled light
of incarnation and renown.

MOON II

traces of my history appear
in your glow, but then fade
in the reflections of light,
angular form, the death
of a star whose

name I once recalled.
this is not amnesia but
a forgetting in the conscious
mind, as sweat forms in
the nerve center of the memory.

moon, allow me to
avow this prayer;
searching in your light
I see my face stare back
as if it had nowhere

to turn, no one upon whom
to gain identity. but to
avow this prayer would
mean redemption, a
recursion of the emotions—

a devotion to a God
I cannot possess. let me
darken in your shadow,
lie across the deck in
the long grain of shade.

moon, avow this prayer
only in the recognition
that no utterance can be
conscious testimony,
but a fractured blood

that spills from the
cordage into the waiting
sea, wading to the
horizon, the borderline
beyond my name.

BREATHING THE WORLD

to sleep again after
the mystery of fever,
furor of dreaming ocean.
tropical birds in the psyche
as the eyes close over

the borderlands. finally,
the death of consciousness
out of a restful death—
angels at the threshold,
petrels in the clouds.

breathing the world,
all ambition collapses,
empires die, glory flags.
surrender to the silent music,
to the origins of prayer.

beat back the waves,
beat back the waves
of nightmarish fever,
and let them gently
fold into my bed.

surrender to the angel,
and let the planet revolve
to a revelation of the
revelatory. sleep now,
splitting head, maps

in order, sacred charts
according to their ministration.
sleep now, for the world
will breathe again
in the breathing of the world.

Book One

EARLY LIFE

I. Hymn to the Atlantic

ocean, help me speak
of my trials and troubles,
my sins and errors; help me sing
of the azure, and the orange
horizon I wake to in your bed.
help me frame a language . . .
whether as fact or fiction.

either as fact or fiction,
construct a discourse
for the children
who wander your waves.
Atlantic, breadth and depth,
home of the sunken earth,
cradle of the gigantic eel,

the three-headed monster,
medium to Cathay. expanse
of gray fire, luminous light
of the open sky. so many eons
running through mouths of history,
so many days meeting
the lips of night.

O voice, your roar-song
drives me into the darkness,
to the light of golden Cathay.
what do I have to prove
through your waste, or my waste
as to human excrement?
wake up the death in me

who finds history a horrendous
text upon which to found
a life. wake up the death
in me so that I might utter
a new vision of civilization.
wave upon wave upon wave
light waves and time waves,

God's hands upon your sacred
sheet. passageway to the sepulcher
I seek. passage to India!
form and froth, order and chaos,
timeless stream, contorted by the
storms of the angry maker, and
the hermeneutist who reads

your waves of text. I attempt to
have an immediate and incorruptible
relation to your force-flood,
the calm that exhausts our pursuit,
or the vortex I sink within
in my dream and death wish.
but it is all text and all language—

and only there can we speak
with any hope. hold up my head
by the tigers of your verbal power,
by the serpents of your virile
grammar. the pentacle you
lift to: let me speak!
hold up my head to the night.

II. Passage of the Heart

THE FAMILY

at twenty I cannot
complain about my place
in the world: my four walls
of family form: powerful
matrix and father-weaver,

brothers and sisters to
complement my desires
for the One and my singular
desire for transgression:
to cross the threshold

of family and form
into space and time-space,
oceans and chronometers
of soaring dream:
pentagons, and drifts of

sand. this is
the circle I occupy.
Columbus within,
Columbus, Christ Bearer,
without. but the mantra

of my birth endures
in the wiry grains of
mind into the deep
roots of that ocean
fable. Colombo, dove—

the need to soar and
to war with peace.
I am my own circle—
yet its lines intersect
with others and with that

Great Circle, whose
heart pulse of generations
sustains the living form. . . .
family: to begin with
historical relatedness

and yet to destroy. here is
the complex of all delusions
and illusions: form and
racial order; chaos and
the enigmas of the universe;

splendor and the suffocating
vortex. I tie my boots
to leave for an hour,
but the heart pulse of the
house drives my blood.

DWELLING

this house upon which
I claim my heart
was built with blood and
effort: square-framed,
arcs of window and door,

solid stone, mason's
hands upon each perfect
block, soul in the ribs.
now birds' nests surround us
in the eaves.

who can deny it a place
in the universe? this house,
built with God's will and
the flow of human seed,
sits in the center of

the planet, like Jerusalem.
who can deny it
a condition among the
elements? who can deny it
an outward orientation,

an inner dimension? for
to dwell is to be, to exist
in the world and of the world,
to dwell in heaven or in
hell, but on this earth.

I am the house and the
house is me. we are in
the center of the solar system
for this brief moment,
breathing together

for the prolonged throb
of the memory. the house
thinks for me, and its brain
expands upon the knowledge
of new things. we make

a pact to go out together—
in that spring of death
when nightingales sing
no more. who can deny us
a place in the universe?

REPAST

at table we talk of
Christ and fishmongers,
Genoese trade, or the
craft of weaving—all
manner of discourse,

but mostly Christ and his
example (the Last Supper,
naturally, our focus
of meditation).
I love Christ with

immaculate passion, but
dispute his pacifism.
how can empires
be built on the shoulders
of non-violence?

. . . but then I eat
to forget his pain, to
stir desire in my body,
to erase the hammer blows
against each hand.

repast, food for the
future, corporeal
pleasures in the moment
of exquisite chatter:
the education of the soul.

how can we learn
from him who gave up
history for God's pasture?
how can we know
the vision from the cloud?

ROOM OF THE SEA

I am lucky to be
alone in the solitude
of this single moment
when my compatriots are
jammed head to foot

in the bustling room
of the fifteenth century.
this is my room of the sea:
blue Mediterranean
through the eye of the

wind. it is enough
to stare and be stared
at in return. the room
enters a dialectic
of plenitude. the full

life of the sea in
the midst of squalor. . . .
all books I have
are coated with that blue
light given to

the fortunate dwellers
of this room. my face
is serene in the light
of the first morning prayer—
upon the sea in the

flight of the windfall-
gull. it is a reverie
without fire. it is the
simple speech of perception.
the eyes utter paradise,

as if it had never been
expressed before, or at least
not with that speech
of sight whose first act
is the illumined word.

I practice this each morning.
it is my monastic duty
to the beautiful: raiment
of the gull along its
spoor to heaven.

INFANCY AND MEMORY

I am not so removed
from infancy that I
cannot observe it in
the plain light of experience.
but experience is always

complicated by a memory
that oscillates between
night and day, between
the wounds of the heart
and the strange thrills

of early access. no fact
is uncomplicated by the
constructions of a memory
in the service of truth—
so that all is reflection

and mirage. penetrations
into my first gaze
upon the sea prove futile
because in that
mirror of time

no two seas
exist alike, and the "I"
is a fathom of two moments,
one isolated, the other
forever moving.

I can only say, with
any certainty, I had
a happy youth: but to
reproduce it poses an
impossibility at two poles.

and yet, is it not
apparent that the sea
has never abandoned
its first joy to the
boy who knew only

sky and the ceiling
of mind?
it is the cave
of memory meeting
the cathedral of emotion.

AMBITION I

what do I want from
the world that the world
can give, or do I milk
from the world what I need?
to limit myself to the

frame of myself and
this room, to do so
with no doubts or remorse,
would be impossible and
invidious against

all venture. what do I
need and how do I seek it?
is the seeking enough:
the quest of the first fruit,
the palpable juice of

discovery? no more
beyond the coast of fame,
no more than the
terrible mountain of
sublimity? what do I

need, and what do I want?
how can I ever say sometime
in the future, I have
attained what I intended,
how can I check the lust

that bleeds at my eyes?
can I merely sit here with
this simple beauty
of blue waves laving
the rock shore, turning

to the white gull—floating
now into the twilight?
what do I need that others
reject who walk these
shores of paradise?

paradise, or hell?—
the total orchestration
of the earthly life
in love with the invisible?
what do I seek

at this very moment?
I am called to prayer
and don my simple
garments . . . luckily,
for I repent.

SEEING MARIA

I noticed her among
a sea of bowed faces,
a communion wafer
pursed in her lips, the
light of the stained glass

playing with her black
hair. I was seeing
Maria for the first time,
not being aware that
she had followed me

here from that realm
of perfect forms, or the
text I had written of
the beautiful. I was seeing
Maria and whatever

precondition I possessed
seemed to vanish
in the sight.
there were two breaths
between us, and two sources

of light, and a language
that existed before we
ever met. yet, whatever
there was in that ideal
history was swept

away in the gigantic
presence of the real: here,
we are humble before
nature. seeing Maria,
I opened all doors,

and felt a pathos
for the one I do not know.
this is the image, this is
the light—blind upon
the ocean of primacy.

AMBITION II

the struggle between
nature and the world
beats like a hurricane
in my head: disease,
malice, self-inflicted

wounds and tornadoes
as from hell converge—
strike up in flashes
and bolts of revenge, fear,
and the terror

of the abstract. I am
revising my plan of the self
at every minute:
destroying myself in
order to resurrect

a fresh conception.
here I am given my
chance for the world.
it is handed to me, so
to speak, in a chalice

of God's servant and
confidant. what do I
do? ruin nature in
the face of Maria?
dissolve all relation

with home? discord
plays its harmonies
at my temple. fire in
the hands chars the skin.
who am I to play God?

but disaster there is
in every choice: to sit
here is to die. I thirst
for the invisible forest
at the borders of sea,

for the skies of Cathay:
firmament and future,
hard rock of empire—
the glorious catechism
of the sea!

III. Ode to Memory

I close my eyes, and
beneath the heavens the
consciousness opens to the world.
I open them not from fear
the memory will collapse,
but because it springs to life
in the fields of space.

memory, I give you my
childhood, my family, my room.
though you shield the fact of
first experience, there in the
light of your serene attentions,
emotion surges. the pain of
the discord between nature

and world, the joy of Maria's
dark countenance all translate
into your aura. . . .
even the sharpest pain is made
sharper by memory (my father's
first blow, my mother's curses);
yet without it no life

can be truly lived.
to erase those scars of our
mental skin, even if possible,
would mean destruction of the
species—for we are here to suffer.
look at my own face now,
drawn for fear of ambition,

and the total dissolve of that
dark image haunting my sleep.
it is memory and its
stabs to the heart, bludgeoning
until we live. there, in the
midst of a nightmare of men
without legs, with heads the size

of boulders, memory works
to reconstruct the preternatural:
it is the early image, distorted,
of the icons I saw in church.
and the joy of that image
from paradise, lush gardens
of geraniums, roseate lips.

memory awakens it . . .
dark Maria walks into my
room as if to bear my troubles
away. and the image now,
ferocious in its vibrancy,
takes the form of daydream. . . .
without cultural memory

the race would die out as well.
for we are meant to remember
our collective works and lives:
the evils, the errors, the monstrosities
of our history. the monuments
of our angelic selves. Lucifer's
fall to Satan, Aristotle's

measurements, the Ptolemaic
universe. distance only urges
the desire to know, to recreate, to
revise the text. I close my eyes again
and seek the Mediterranean.
the veil is removed,
and a greater blue I cannot recall.

IV. Imago Mundi

THE WORD

the rite turned
toward leeward
and there before me
stood God: white radiance,
holy water in one hand,

dark beard. he told me
of lands never visited
by contemporary man,
but once known to Polo,
Prester John, and their kin.

a sepulcher is hidden
there, in a great monastery
in Cathay, at the lowest
point where the sea
can be heard in the land.

there, in a golden chalice,
sits the Word, unadorned,
pure, immutable, and
dynamic. it is yours,
so to speak, to decode.

here is the key to the
chalice, here instructions
for decoding—the magnificent
Word, the Word of God,
the Word of apocalypse.

translate it and you
will save souls, and
end war for all time.
I have nothing more to
say. Amen.

in a brilliant wind,
folded by the blue sea
beneath him, he was
gone. I stood, exhausted,
trembling—

my entire body
sweating. the rite
turned toward leeward,
and for the first time
my heart pulsed—*mysterium*.

DESTINY

it was a miracle, of
course, but was it
miraculous? was it
a virginal experience
or a member of that

prehistory written
out in a text
before birth? who can
utter this language,
who knows its grammar?

what are the roots
of this holy message
come, by surprise, at
the very moment
I had sworn off ambition?

—and yet another text.
and yet another.
the Word of God
imprinted on my soul,
but was it miraculous?

who was the first
to read the hidden
moment of my
light? and could
they tell if I were

destined for this later
light? who could tell me
now? and yet another
text, and yet another.
but was it miraculous?

was it Maria's text
whose image speaks
more eloquently than
prayer?—it was
another text: no love

could trust the world
of voyage-sea. it was
another.—I comb through
words, the syllables of air:
was it miraculous?

AMBITION III

in the visit of the
sacred one, in these
questions of destiny,
what is ambition? can
I alter my "I" to

subjugate the drive
for future, for unknown
worlds, for dynamos
of cosmic space? and even
if I tried, is there any

"I" to speak of, now that
I have been touched
by him forever?
surrender to the
indelible nexus

of fate and events.
love will have
to wait at the
threshold between sea
and shore as Cathay

calls in its golden
orchestration. Maria's
eyes scald my flesh—
but I cannot stay—
lady love, wait,

for I cannot stay who
thirsts for the buried
text of Cathay. drive,
drive on, substitute
desires for the treasure

of the incorrigible Word,
drive on, importunate
echo in my heart. I
hunger for the manifold
wealth of language,

for a world I search
to map. carry my
drive into the ships
of superhuman voyage,
into the seaworthy vessels

of the blessèd Trinity.
search and discover . . .
landlocked and
fallow, I plunge
into the laving foam!

A HISTORY OF MY LIFE AT SEA

in a violent storm
when rains lashed
against the memory
and all were abed
after the last prayer

(and death walked
into the house of dreams),
I recall the first time
fishing on shore, gulls
dipping out of voluminous

clouds. it was before I
broke my fear with the sea.
a mystical man, a farmer
turned fisherman next
to me, spoke of the imminent

disorder of his lands,
how he must fish
until a magical feeling
in his body returned him there.
his eyes were glassy

on the blue waves.
finally, I broke my
fear with the sea and rode
sloops off the coast. a short
leap later, I took my

first caravels to Iceland,
Norway, where I spoke
with Viking-fabulists,
and to the coast of Brittany.
in a moment's pulse,

I was swimming for
my life, a wound
bleeding through the sea,
when the French exploded
our desires. there

I found Portugal and
Henry the Navigator—
the project of conquest
and discovery. the waves
fell over my bleeding body.

in a myth-dream
I swam the breadth
of the Styx and met the shade
of my dead uncle, Antonio,
who taught me all about

the sea. he warned me,
to delay would be
catastrophic, a blow
to the text of history—
which he read with

astute care, a hermeneutist
of the first magnitude.
while there, I called on
Ulysses to relate his
exploits of the sea,

how he navigated
the problem of Scylla
and Charybdis, fought off
sweet Circe and
overcame the monster

Cyclops while all along
dreaming, nostalgically,
of Penelope and the
kingdom of his house.
could Maria learn

from this paradigm of
patience, the shroud
woven as if it were a
life work? hail Penelope,
these wounds to the heart.

and surfacing I came to
the ocean shore, the Ocean Sea
in the scope of my eyes.
my ship, a golden vessel
of state, ready for sail.

a crew of ninety,
hail, hearty, young to
old, inveterate and
novitiate, servants and
bellicose men of the sea.

and we embarked onto
the weather of prayer,
Ave Maria, holy dare,
sea shaking, waves
in our eyes . . . we

swaddled in that brine
and blue . . .
until the storm off the
Mediterranean foists its
world of wind and toil

into our house, and the
house shuddered with such force
that I thought I heard
the curse of the builder,
in the first flood of God.

SOURCES OF LIGHT

who was the first
to show me that sun
whose light rises in
faraway provinces,
like a plate of gold

with a circle of
spurting beams?
I awake in the dawn
and in the first splendid
light on my table

wonder, who was the
first to lead me to
the East? God, of course,
with his hands cast out
into that sun,

but who was the first
to lead me East
through the portals of
the Western gate? d'Ailly,
Pliny, Ptolemy, Aristotle?

who was the first, or
was there a text of the
light as well? to go East,
West seems strange,
even to me, who hear

myself speak at court
with such conviction.
a curious idea for one
with his feet on the ground.
but is it not obvious, in fact?—

for the water-world
is not so large as they
have made us believe.
I consult them all, and
Polo's estimate of Cathay—

its proximity to the West—
and it all screams, yes—
it must be. in the first
light, in the first sun,
it is there where

all things meet.
in its opposition rests
conjunction . . . in the golden
light a sign of nirvana . . .
imperium; *mysterium*.

AT THE COURT OF ISABELLA

it was she who
understood my desire
immediately—after many
years, that is, many
years of my "courting"

the sovereigns on their
own ground. what
finally broke the
veil between us,
so that she could grasp

the simplicity of the
concept? the beauty of
its plainness thrown
aside by doubting men
on high, the Thomases

of state? I often
wondered, after that
final acceptance, did she
know from the beginning
to trust my desire,

but could not agree,
despite her interest,
because of Ferdinand?
because of Ferdinand
and his kind who

believe only the palpable?
not that I did not
have science behind me,
in the shade of my
cloak, or the purest

proofs of philosophy.
what they could not
understand was the
invisible of science, the
visionary path to unseen

zones: thought, imagination,
and the life of risk
embraced by the inventive
rebel. and I was foreign,
a Genoese sailor, and no more.

not even a formal
education by which
to demonstrate my argument.
but she knew, at least
later, I had truth on my

side, and our eyes met
as if to say we are
brother and sister
of the dangerous unknown,
we are one of a kind.

she had enough charm
to convince Ferdinand,
the council powers, and all
of Spain from the ocean
to the sheep fields.

I will be forever beholden . . .
but enough, I must away!
before the doubters have
their way in the world—
and our magic is crushed.

V. Maria's First Monologue

when we first met—our eyes,
that is—in church, I
knew you were deluded
by a pre-image of me: your
male fantasy of beauty in
the abstract. I became
aware all at once that if there

were to be any future between
us, you had to be purged
of that ideal. I could sense
from your eyes in their transport
and in the wound you wore
around them of previous failure,
it was hardly me you were

seeing, but a phantom you
had created in your active
psychic life, drawing upon a
long history of disillusion,
a male fund of female distortions.
I was in love at first sight
also, but not because I

had seen you in a previous
existence, a Columbus constructed
out of a catalogue of images,
a female equivalent of your
flesh and blood icons. it
was because I was attracted
to the vision your eyes had

settled on and which
all the light of them had
folded around. it was the magic,
not the image, I was struck by
and that powerful sense of the
otherworldly you carried
even as you seemed to reject it.

now that we are married, it
has taken all my force to
destroy the ideal Maria and
to replace her with the
real life of pain and anguish—
and of a joy that comes not out
of ether but out of the belly

of existence: a love made of
the fractures and the epiphanies
of earth. as you embark on
your first voyage of discovery
and meet the Other across the
ocean, beware this false ideal
and make peace with difference;

allow for the reality of their
world—an ancient history
of the collective and free.
new man, Columbus, heed my words,
but smother your text of me,
the ideal for the real, true love
for the veil . . . the Other.

Book Two

THE FIRST VOYAGE

I. Hymn to Cathay

I lift my cup to you, Cathay;
with you I have a pact
through God. it is the Word
I seek in your deepest core,
your sepulcher of the splendid
text. there to decode and bring
myself glory, the end of war,

and the honor of him I worship
with such troubling love.
Cathay, locus of gold, fine
silks, minerals and spices;
spatial dream of rivers and
plains; stone bridges lined
with marble. land of

humble people with gracious
manners; civilized cities;
industry and commerce
superior in all the world.
rivers too broad to carry
bridges; so many ships for
trade . . . Cathay,

I seek your gold—
there too beneath your
thunderous beauty to trade
my Christian mien for
the gold of Khan. I sing you
anthems of prayer and a chorus
of the one God, whose true

Word will bless you
with the benefits of his
humble heaven. Cathay,
Eastern miracle, convergence
of all opposites, I seek
completion in your Other.
as the sun rises from the golden

dome at the door of your Ocean,
I seek your primal light. . . .
from the cave of the Word
and the caverns of precious
gold, to the height of that
first light—and now God—
I seek myself.

II. Voyage of Discovery

SHIPS OF STATE

these three ships,
a token of the love
of kings, entrusted
with the noble duty of
the state, with God's

imperative, the history
of the race. for we have
come to this; and I am
the force field through
which our destiny gains

fruition. Spain stands
above Portugal at this
hour, for why sail the
hot seas south—around
Africa and the Arabian

waters beyond?
I will quiet the doubters
and cross West from
Palos to Cathay, from
shore to shore unsailed

before. it is in the
stars, as they say, and
whatever ruinous doubts
I myself possess at
the threshold of this voyage,

through the burden of my
psychic history, when
folded in the arms
of Maria, have vanished—
at least subsided—

for at this moment
I feel a captive
of fate, a prisoner
of these ships of time,
whose itinerary

is set for no mere
island in the sea
but for the quantum leap,
the space-time coordinates
of a larger design.

sail seas and conquer
ports of call above
the drift of tide and scum.
sail into the oasis of
the unimagined beyond.

THE EXPULSION OF THE JEWS

as luck would have it,
all Jews were ordered
to relinguish Spain
(or their God) by the
date we sailed for Cathay.

our blustery white, hopeful
in the predawn light, passed
the last ghostly vessel of
the meandering Jews—they tossed
from their houses with few

worldly possessions;
the rest remained for
Spain. history has only
so much room for its
victors; the others suffer

ignominy. . . . to refuse the
Christian hegemony meant
expulsion, denial of the
protections of state,
and, like the Moors,

eternal exile from
the Christian heaven.
—a loss, to be sure,
and only the proud could
refuse Spain and its

beautiful God. forlorn,
the vessel sailed into the
rising August sun, a cursed
people riding out their
cursed seas. we were

gloating about our
blessèd state, illumined
by God's light on the
windsail sea, a *Salve
Regina* to the skies. . . .

yet, how could we outstrip
this blemish in our history;
how counter the Jews'
total humiliation—
outcasts on a sea whose

course, the very same as
ours, ran into the
dark dungeons of ignorance
and starvation, their
nature denuded, roots all

mangled of their sanctity?
how could we call our voyage
destiny when others were
destined to doom? how
could we claim our rights

to the world when
others were exiled?
I stand on the deck of the
rising light hoping
for answers. it is history,

I think, that seeks
the path of our Savior—
the sublime sweep of our
fledgling ships, while
others sail to disgrace.

ITINERARY OF FEAR

sail South, I order
and then West
until we touch
the golden domes of
Cipangu. a short stop

at the Canaries and
then on to Cathay.
avoid the northerlies
for the spices of India!
here the stars are

magnificent: Polaris,
and the three faithful.
astrolabe at work,
but useless: all
dead reckoning ahead.

now the Ocean is boundless
upon us: no one before
has witnessed these
waves: blue-green . . .
a blue tapestry

of sky. this is the
history upon which
we sail, this is God's
universe—a vast sea
beckoning us,

the raw firmament
of stars. where will
it lead us who have
never come this way,
where will it end?

how do we name
ourselves in such infinity?
sky, ocean, the indifferent
species in the waves?
a terror sets in,

but I cannot surrender . . .
and yet this leap
makes us great who
dare to face the terror,
the nameless future

of the stars. here
we move in eternal
time, the faith
of uncertainty,
the realm of the

pioneer. this is
our destiny: humble
in God's order,
rash in the
splendid waves.

LETTER TO MARIA

I want to express
my love anew, Maria,
lady of the dark eyes
and hair, whose
darkness rings

such brilliance
around my life.
when I put you off
in those last days
it was in order to come here,

here in this white
emptiness, and to
separate myself from
land and love. I could
not have borne the

transition had I held onto
the earth. my love,
you must understand
this as I see again
the wound in your eyes.

our marriage means
more than sea and air
and the vast breadth
of this Ocean; but this
project goes beyond me,

a voyage to the absolute,
God's home.
it is the Word
I seek, no mere
adventure for the sake

of the sea's
marvels. understand
that my ground is you
and your beauty; my
desire reaches for your

face. I kiss you entire.
but the white emptiness
calls now—the impersonal,
the abstract, the universe
in its uncaring magnitude.

finally a fever that
has blocked my vision
has passed and I
look into the sea brine
and find the outlines

of your face: I hold
the image through
the speechless cosmos:
come with me . . . but in
flesh I must go alone.

THE MIND'S MUTINY

in all my wanderings
I have come to discern
those who would dare
and those who doubt: the
two meeting in life in the

voyage that engulfs us.
one has a single mind,
a conviction that wipes
out the brutal grin
of death; the other

wavers between action
and a rest that unnerves
him. I am the first,
but doubt paws at me
like a hungry dog.

it is the first I show
to the world in order
that it understands my
position, my soul's pure
desire: the very roots

of my singular feeling
for the unknown. it is
those who doubt this
enterprise and the
end to this Ocean

who grumble, and who,
I think, drive
daggers into my spine
when I face the sea.
the others ride waves—

113

like Poseidon rising
from the depths, throbbing
in the joy of the
imagined-invisible.
I embrace them

as brothers of the sea,
a fellowship
that shares a gangplank
with death.
and to the doubters

I say, I am
determined to find
Cathay, and no one—
no one—will stop me
from that quest.

BETWEEN DESIRE AND LANDFALL

last night I saw
a light off starboard
and thought it was land,
but passed it off
to bad eyes.

today a sailor spotted
land but I took the
prize: the light was
my desire and I deserved
whatever I could get

from it. it was my urge
that brought us here,
my drive. let the doubters
in Spain besmirch my
proposal, but no one

can destroy the promise
between my heart and
mind. those theoreticians
of the Negative can
eat sand now!

my desire overtakes
doubt, and what I see
I see with the force of God.
it is land ahead, my land,
and what I name

belongs to my desire.
landfall! what joy
in the golden men who
think our ships from
heaven . . . Cathay,

kingdom of islands
and mainland . . . this
very day my desire
gives rise to San Salvador,
and now Christendom rises

from its grave. O noble
Ferdinand and Isabella,
your empire emerges
from the depths of the
ocean floor: a new

Spain born of my desire,
the Word of God
carried on the backs
of slaves. . . . let me now
tell you of this island-earth.

here the sea meets land
with such a gentle touch
that all the islanders
seem born of its innocence:
they are your keep.

III. Ode to History

in the dark spaces of time,
before recorded text, life was
lived without the breath of
consciousness. instead, there
was the breath of the elements—
fire, water, earth, and air—
all inscribed within creative

nature; and we knew through
mythos. this was before myth
was transmuted through epic
singers into written form:
the miraculous remaking
of the universe. for though myth
persisted, history found its

form in the text of life. . . .
history, everything is
transformed within you,
subservient to the theory of
knowledge you represent: the
story of our voyage on God's
earth; magic and disaster;

good and evil; the fall
and the redemptive urge.
text of the one life and the
many, I call on you
because you are the act,
the force of change, the powerful
earthquake of epochs.

how can we determine
our fate without you? how
can we make a claim of the earth
without the lightning rod of
your future?—as if not to exist,
not to exist without the vengeance
of your text . . .

the heirs of history would
also die out without your
remarkable testimony.
if we remember—but without
you we would surely forget.
to forget is the comfortable
death into which we fall—

the bad dream we have
inherited from the past.
but to forget means an
even worse dream: a living
Golgotha repeated again
and again until our agony
becomes almost unbearable.

I want to be a verb in
your living text, an actor
on your stage, whose sword
takes flight into the
stratosphere of future.
listen to this history,
listen to the text I write

with the blood of my
deeds. lift up this nightmare,
lift up: for history contains
the seed of a new history.
even as the past swallows us,
we write with the flaming
text of the new.

IV. The Other

BRIDGING

upon this crossing,
a liminal passage
between two points of
time and space, a permanent
bridge came to be between

continents and cultures:
two great civilizations
forever bound in transport
and trade, in intercourse
of manners and customs,

in the sharing of soil
and race, to the roots
of their genesis: histories
interlocked in the fluid
passage of the cosmos.

for we now share those
stars that signify the
fate of the planet; and
the waters that flow
between us are the one Ocean

of God's ship. hail
these three ships that
sailed the green dream
of reverie: nirvana of
the One Mind that gave

us thought. beautiful
flow of the waters and
skies between us: bridge
of iron and gold and the
natural order of his gift. . . .

I find myself humbled
in the great consciousness
now shared between these
kingdoms of the earth:
I drink the water of the bay

and think it Spain; I take
my vows at compline, and
worship the God of Cathay.
we hold hands, my Indian
and I, in a brother embrace

of love on the bridge of
our earthly voyage. here
rises that span, arc of
waves and blood: we walk
across the waters of our sage.

ADMIRATION OF THE VISIBLE

when Adam and Eve
first walked the earth,
they must have admired
the many things about them:
trees and animals and

streams, all such that
they partook of his Creation
and created with their eyes.
it was that primal light—
the flood upon them—

that swam in their veins
and in their brain,
which gave all things
a freshness and a beauty:
they were in such

a relation to the world
that it was not they
and the world so much
as a world
of which they were a part.

a miraculous linking
of the light and the world
and their flesh and blood,
in a harmony of subject
and object.

such intersections, I
would think, that a
music swelled between
them. it is in this light
I see the Indies, but

without the innocence
of that first fame. I have
no naked body with which
to claim these things—like
them whose primal light

mirrors the harmony
of our ancestors. naked
in the world they go
as if to utter a compact
between forms: human

and nature in such
explicit desire of one
another: all eyes upon the
visible and the resplendent
manifold, the various

flora and fauna—
the simple conditions
of this life-stream. my
Indians will teach us
something of these wonders,

how to live our parents'
lives again: magic of
nature and human in a
a correspondence of the visible,
in a new history of primacy.

TERRA FIRMA

firm land after the
abstract sea: many
weeks of a mutation
of mind: ethereal concord
and discord in the blue

infinity. earth again,
mother of all things,
enfolding us in the
curvatures of brown and green.
for this is reality

upon which we step,
the natural habitat
of speech. yet the sea
is my strange dominion
and I suffer the land

whose very solidity
unnerves me. motility
of oars or sails, mobile
waves, changing skies:
this is the flux upon which

I constitute my life.
it is in its dangers that
I soar: the uncertainties
of its tides, the crescendos
of storms.

but terra firma calls
upon which we claim
our deaths—and now
our empire in the East!
I dig in the roots

of its soil to find
the Word: Cathay,
where is your chalice
of the sacred text,
how do I probe your many

islands without benefit
of language? for we do
not speak, those who
know the land to the
stomach of the mother;

and even signs for gold
have proved futile.
Juana, go to Juana
and the sail gods take us
there, but no chalice,

no monastery of the
Word. O holy mother,
give us the signature
of your earth upon
which to decipher his text.

take us to the tomb.
there in the heart
of terra firma next to
the breath of the sea,
the Word vibrates eternally.

THE DEATH OF THE SANTA MARIA

the earth gave back
its anger, moved toward
us like a tidal wave:
it hoped to swallow us as
in the hubris of Greek tragedy.

mother of the soil, forgive us
who have trod upon you,
indignant passengers
from the sea. Santa Maria is
grounded in the middle of

the night, dark riddle in
our chests, Santa Maria
grounded while I slept.
only the boy to blame,
but I in the end must bear

the guilt. mother of the
soil, forgive us who have
trespassed . . . and from its
timber we build *La Navidad* . . . I have
come here, mother, and will stay.

TEMPEST AND WINTER'S WORLD

in the dark days of
our return, with Spain
a distant mirage, nature
has risen in wild waves
and wind, torrential against

our sails, cold rains
flooding upon our bare heads.
bare poles scudded we
sail, or try to, barely
moving ahead against

voluminous air: a taste
of God's wrath, this,
for failing to keep his
compact. I promise every
night with prayer to do

better the next voyage,
and we all take oaths of
pilgrimage. onward
men, fight seas, for we
have witnessed such

wonder with our eyes!
we bring no Word
but the ringing perception
of these undiscovered
isles: the gems of new

Spain! onward through
fierce winter and our
bitter tears. let us preach
to the theoreticians of
the Negative about these pearls.

gold in our eyes who
saw these lands: the
luminous light of the
once invisible. now thunder
and lightning foil

our discourse of the miraculous.
all speech fails in
the thunderous discord of
his wrath. will winds
come with waves uplifting

to capsize these happy
vessels? will the tragic
bolts electrocute the comic
dream? I cannot face my
death without the message

flowing through, flow
through cask unto the
beach of the brilliant
shore. flow through so
we may all be remembered.

RESTLESS TRIUMPH

why are there some who
sit or stand in place,
happy to do no more,
while others are eternally
restless? I stand

at court with the glories
and souvenirs of my
conquest and am anxious
to move, move and never
stop. yet, in my moment of

triumph, I am content to
gloat at the theoreticians
of the Negative; for West
it will be from here to
the infinite shore; and West

it will be to the banks of
kingdom come. it is my fate
to walk these seas, to steer
God's ship into the mad dream.
I have no home but in the

floating carcass of these
rigs. O give me sea, lust
of the metaphysical blue . . .
for to stand here longer
means death!

V. Maria's Second Monologue

yes, my eyes were wounded,
as you say; and I turned
myself into a nun for three
weeks, not knowing where
to turn for comfort.
your heart hardens for
the task, mine darkens.

I am here, nevertheless,
with love in my body:
all rapture and irony.
when you come, I will be
yours again, but the light
will have changed in my eyes
unless you make a vow

to the unremitting icon of
our love. you move like
waves, you say, and need
time to settle into my beauty.
but there is a danger you will
spin wearily out of time
on the tidal wave you claim

to praise, the awesome
constructions of God's Creation.
one can make a world in
the house of the body, out of
limits, if the mind plies hard
with what it has: a world
of the magic fable of two lovers

in the sea of the real.
you claim to be as real
as any man, but there is
a problem in your words,
a hesitation in your voice;
for your real is in the capricious
waves, in the evaporating sky,

and the sun stands in the
house of the mind. it is
apparent in the way you have
dealt with the Other of your first
voyage, imagining them to be
servants of our Queen majesty,
malleable for our Christian quest;

and how you have imposed
your standards upon them
as if they were Spaniards
with beards instead of naked
innocents. I fear calamity
will befall them, such hell
and horror: I foresee this

in the gap between our worlds.
it is in your power to see
them for what they are and
to respect the world they
have made out of the wisdom
of nature. for you will kill
nature also if you kill them,

and the glow of history
now upon you will unravel
in a dark terrible storm.
my heart will take you back
and my body will throb in
yours (probably for the rest
of our lives), but in my eyes

you will perceive this
warning on your return.
in the narrative of our love,
I can forgive you. but beyond
the margins of our lives,
there in the hallowed light,
you will be judged.

Book Three

THE SECOND VOYAGE

I. Hymn to Hispaniola

any island survives
of its own life, fronting
the sea: heroic solitude,
fortitude against the massive forces
of God's machine-like universe.
Hispaniola, you assume this
destiny with such grace and

beauty, an entire cultural
life set upon your massive
frame. for you are more
spacious than Spain, wide
as the Tagus, and rise from
the sea on the backs of elephants.
Hispaniola, theater of the new

Spain, the stage of a cultural
renaissance. for we breed
new life on your shores, up
and down the spine of the Valley
of Paradise, and in the roots
of your splendid forests.
new conditions for the

Christian text culminate
in your peoples, white as the
race of Spain, except for the
sun on their naked skin.
Hispaniola, lovely oasis
in the storm of God's madness,
bounteous harbors and plains,

bedrock of gold, streams
that flow with mineral ore,
green dream against the
recumbent shore. azure skies
raise you to the meadows of heaven.
star-clad, your nights
conduce to love. here,

on the beaches of your
blessèd shore, a new man
emerges, father of a new age
and race, who will spell
your name in the text of
destiny: Hispaniola, he beams,
you will sleep in paradise.

I. Imperial Dream

STATELY POWER

my mind is full of the
sails of state, seventeen
ships, fifteen hundred
men: architects of destiny.
such abundance to weave

the text of the new man,
vision and power in a
complex semantics. for
to be honest, do we not
own the universe,

we who gave God his
name? we who rule
nature with our science?
look at the silver in
this watery desert

jump at our prow.
look at the cormorants
soar to miss our masts.
such majesty could not
exist of nature alone;

and the state rises
above the crucible of God
when God is weak.
for to be honest, can we
not own the heavens

if we wished? I stand
at the helm of the
seventeen sublime,
the Ocean Sea in our pocket,
a miracle of human dream:

where can we sail
when all sailing's done,
where can we fly such
majesty? these are
flags of state

waving their signatures
over the savage seas,
these are the semiotics
of power: who can
contest them?

THE PROBLEMATICS OF EXPERIENCE

will experience ruin
the primacy of our quest,
our first crossing
extinguish the majesty
of peril? how do we

recuperate the dialectical
tension with his master's
domain? to have done once
dissolves the pure need.
what force in us can stir

the flames of first
desire? it is like a
woman's body we have
navigated in the seas of time,
conquest impossible

unless storms swell up
to break the peace. then
the intense pain reproduces
the radiance of first
encounter when shyness

reigns over our nakedness.
it is stormy nature we
rule with that desire,
our challenge to the God
whose thirst is dictatorial

power. let these green seas
blow up against our
caravels. let the winds upset
the crest of our arrogance.
we stand to win by

the ascension of death.
cast out our tired bodies
to the shores of Cathay.
cast out: apocalypse
sings in our chests!

PASSAGE TO PARADISE

alas, calm seas,
trade winds at our
disposal, such easy
passage to paradise. the
Caribbees call in their

sensual fruits. new
discoveries and marvels
assuage us. these are people
I must rule: clothe them,
teach them our terce and

compline, our paradisal
construction of the text.
is this Cathay? . . .
what fools these people are
who speak a language of pure

nature. how can we know
the world without its
written forms, how can
we claim a paradise
without a text of the beautiful? . . .

I must enslave them,
for to make them useful
as Christian vessels,
they will need to learn
the pain of manacles.

THE CANOE

from island to island
we teach the language
of power. discourse of
reality: the weak belong
to the strong. it is

nature we say that gave
us this bequest—and it is
we who preach its
oracle of the master and
slave. let us kneel to

the tabernacle of the Word—
with fire in our chests,
let us destroy in order
to create. and we round
up slaves to be happy

pilgrims of our power,
to learn the language
of our violent syntax.
to own them for their own
good and to own

the lush land whose
beauty they never understood.
yes, this is the language
of the world's way
and we teach it through

the prayers of duty.
God grant us the heart
to stave off the doubters
in their canoe who stare
for a blue hour of wonder,

struck by our seventeen
ships from heaven—raw
power—testimony of the
awesome text. what could
they imagine who lack

the language of imagination?
power makes right,
turns darkness to light,
enhances the hope for immortality.
imperial dream, imperial dream . . .

I am riding your carpet
to the sublime . . .
the Indians are undone by
their own means—surreptitiously—
as they stare like children

onto the citadels of state.
awestruck, they suffer
the machinations of power:
bow and arrow against machine.
one we need to kill

three times, his guts hanging
foul. in this hour of the
contest of cultures, it is
the language of our God
that rings the seas.

REPRISAL IN HISPANIOLA

when I saw the mountains
rising like a woman's breast,
I knew I was entering
the paradise of power.
we kissed the shore,

all seventeen of our royal
fleet. where were our men
of *La Navidad* to greet us?
our men who had undertaken
this epic enterprise?

power makes right,
turns darkness to light,
enhances the hope for immortality.
dead, we were told,
butchered by these

so-called innocents
for raping their women,
filching their gold,
(gentle, I thought them)
all forty and the fort destroyed.

Lucifer, Satan, light
of eternal hell . . . did
they act rashly in order
to serve the state? I call
upon your powers to

negotiate. I turn to
you for the justice of
the sword. Satan, Lucifer,
God of the firelight,
luminous master—what to

do with this grieving
passion I restrain? . . .
O Cathay, I lament
our Christian blood
has stained your Word.

III. Ode to Power

between despair and doubt,
I coil up in your python force
and destroy the enemies of
my soul. we read your name
in bold text across the tumid seas.
we read your violent language:
Logos and logic, the splendid

rawness of your verbs. power,
take me into your ferrous veins
who brood of tragedy in the
land. give my blood a
stinging vibrancy to poison
the detractors of our text. for we
worship the pure venom of

your febrile language,
the destructive forces
embedded in its interstices.
even death worships at your
door whose threshold yields
the sign of the red fang.
you conquer love's delicacies

for the iron mission of the
state. power, uncoil your
volcanic lava at my heart
where it will burn the remnants
of forgiveness. overwhelm the
weak who stare crazed at your
menacing demeanor, Cyclops

crushing all beauty. we
read the rhetoric of your
text as the sacred code
upon which to rule, upon
which to act out our demonic
desires. it is your great head
we give homage to for its

sickly thoughts. evil
incarnate, logic of war-force,
cancer to the weak body,
deleterious force upon the
innocent who read no text.
we read and worship the words
that bury them under your shoes.

IV. Imperial Conquest

A VISION

there is thunder in
my cabin and lightning
without storm, a quaking
without rain or hail,
a sudden shock and

all spins as if it would
leave the earth. the
midday sun rises
before me in my subterranean
cell: I am captive of

its oppressive power:
beating, beating, beating
in this season without heat.
it sends a shock of light
through my body and

I am incandescent, about
to burn as if on a funeral
pyre. God forgive this
wicked wastrel. it is
only then as I tremble

and thirst for a drop
of water, that I see
the sign beyond the
terror. a metallic
crystalline of ore,

a bronze stream of
marvellous shine.
O brilliance that overtakes
me, O lust for the sun
that brightens to vaporous

steam. I lie abed
and my whole body
assumes the yellow
lightning of the sun,
a furnace within which

to melt the minions.
auriferous sun that
sweeps me up into the
alchemical tower: there
I manufacture my earth.

there I transform
the clay into a brilliant
urn. sun, light the
way to the inner mysteries
of this spectral dream.

A THEORY OF THE STATE

flags flying now from
Isabela, new fortress
of the new Spain: the
new man throws his signs
down, and they take seed

as swords of gold.
gold and the text of
the imperial quest: the
textualization of power
and the rhetoric of state.

for providence is implicit
in the language of blood
and gold, and history
gains immortality in
the word. in the word,

for written we have power
and myth dies on our swords.
the feeble become
denizens of our towers
where the signs of the

new man ring true.
there Spain articulates
its sources, authors its
vision of the future,
composes its lexicon.

there the state achieves
the language of destiny.
for in its shores the
racial magnitude flaunts
its passion for design.

now the text is ready
for the sign's dissemination:
here power pulses
in the bloody signature,
here the golden sword

sears its mark across
the weak. O holy
python, crush the
oral throat of those
who cannot write.

THE ETHICS OF SLAVERY

even Aristotle
condoned slavery, and
to be fair, all men are
slaves of one sort or
another: slaves of mothers,

slaves of wives, slaves
of the state. and women
by their very nature are
slaves. we wake at birth
with manacles at our hands,

chains at our feet:
prisoners of nature
or of the human
condition, prisoners
without hope or volition.

only a very few of us can
muster such force
to break these natural
bonds, or the social
burdens that sink

or crush us. God himself
has put in us the seed
of the weak, and we become
his human servants
whose very doubts

are checked by our fear
of hell and damnation:
eternal fire, and fishes
we are forced to swallow
from his river of phlegm . . .

power makes right,
turns darkness to light,
enhances the hope for immortality . . .
so why these doubts,
my King and Queen,

you who rule thousands
of vassals and a vast
army? the Indians are
ripe for such labor,
practically thirst to be

Christian slaves. let
us make them pilgrims
of our text, let us work
their bodies to the lean
spirit of our Testament.

enslave them, I say!
for they have nothing
better to do, and the
capital we gain from
their bodies can help

build Christian monuments,
fortresses and ships,
new languages of discord.
and we will conquer Islam
once again!

the python slides from
bay to shore, hungering
for the weak: raw nature
overtakes the impotent—
strangulation . . . surcease.

PRIMAL GOLD

the gold embedded
in the land belongs to us
and we must take it.
mother lode of the state:
Spain at the source of

creation. this at all
cost, for we cannot let
destiny perish in our
tardiness, our delays.
push nature to the limits,

push all manner of men,
women, and children to
the effort. drive them with
whips and dogs, let our
curs swallow the hands

of those who disobey.
it is in the mother that
we see the light of
the future: yellow filaments
of utopian towers,

roofs and rivers
of auriferous dream.
mother, give us back
the riches of our labors,
we who have journeyed

in vessels from heaven,
we who see with laser eyes
into the night. make them
wear tokens, those who
contribute; those who

do not will be killed.
cut off their hands, I suggest.
the others will follow
with streams of gold.
rich rainbows of dust

and metals, necklaces
for the Queen, chalices
for our cathedrals: beauty
of ritual, beauty of the
court in its theater of

power. holy mother,
render your gifts—
our slaves for your asking—
unto the missionaries
of the destined dream.

THE EARTH OF CHRISTENDOM

before the morning rosary,
the winter sun beaming
on our sails—as if through
a religious reverie, the land,
I felt, belonged to us

as well. *repartimientos*
for the Spanish Christians
who have dared the seas:
the earth of Christendom.
here we will build and enslave

and privatize, absorb the
entire East, mesmerize the world . . .
O Christendom, I am your bearer
across the wild Atlantic,
I carry you to the savage hearts

of these unfortunate supplicants:
for your earth extends now
from streams of gold
to the rainbow of heaven.
hail to our Lord,

master of the text of power
(it is his Word I seek
in the secret soil). hail . . .
from fallow to fertile
we till this earth of blood.

RETURN AND REVIEW

. . . and then we head back,
our ships down to two,
hungry as poor lambs
on the heath. how could
we accommodate so many

who were longing for Spain?
even the ocean seemed beset
by our weight (two hundred
and fifty five, all told) . . .
it is destiny's fate

to be ridiculed for the
love of one's birth; it is
the visionary that will be
cast down for the known.
or is it the Word

and my failure to find it
that has clipped our sails?
no, the Power will reign
in our absence, there in
the land of the fulgent

sun, ready to shower
gold on the ancient soil;
the text will rule over the
primitive element; the
terrible-visionary will

conquer; the python will
crush. they will see, at
last, the shining verbs
of the text of destiny,
there in the bloody flag

157

of state, when gold and
pearls spring to life
and spices flood from
the mountains. they will see
again but not now

because they are hungry
and provisions are low.
they are hungry and are
ready to eat the slaves,
cannibals, no less than

the Caribs of the Indies.
so we are rooted in
our stomachs after all
and our visions
will have to wait . . .

alas, land ahead,
the home of the tiring
angels. Lord, I will
walk in your shadows
and master the love of my hate.

V. Maria's Third Monologue

it will be difficult
to love you now, but I
will try. night after night
I have nightmares
of the severed hands
and the curious look
on the faces of the innocent

who stagger away surprised
they are leaving this life.
how could you consent to such
slaughter, such demonism to
pluck from the land the little
gold it possesses? for you know
as well as I there is barely

enough gold in the Indies
to make a medallion, and
that Cathay breathes many
thousands of miles from its
shores. Columbus, I beg you
to open your eyes to this genocide,
and to the sick dream of wealth

and domination fastened as a
burden on their backs. for it
is an act of perception along
with the moral dimension
involved in the facts as they
exist, and your perception
is skewed by the sun-drenched

aura of gold. I see the
sun in your head radiating
over the mountains and the
river streams, luminous
rondure of destruction,
cathode of dementia,
working its way into every

pore of your dream. it will
electrocute your Cathay,
burn in its lightning the
monastery of the Word and
leave you hungering for more
flesh of gold. this I see
with the clarity of a god,

though I remain humble before
all superhuman intervention.
perhaps our love will wake
your eyes to the apocalypse
of gold, to the pitiful Indians
forced to surrender their world
and their lives in the most stupid

of deaths, barbaric civilization.
Columbus! look into my heart
again and slip into this love
I strain to keep alive. for you
will go mad as sure as the
cock crows on your devastated
lands: that fallen paradise.

Book Four

THE THIRD VOYAGE

I. Hymn to the Indies

O lands that rise
out of God's sea, never
known before to human
mind, invisible on the maps
of the great geographers;
another work in the great
text of history whose first words

go back to the work of his
Creation. for it is by my
invention that you exist
and all your rivers empty into
my sea. O glorious Indies,
such paradigms of place,
such jewels in the palpable

universe of the earth—
yet you are the terrestrial
sublime we are all longing
for as well. it is there
in the nether realms of my
image-making place, the
dark creative origins of

all fertile dream that
you came to me, rising
upward to find the magic
light, and now ascending
from those seas of God's love.
such is the sublime that
it dwells within, as beauty,

your golden streams,
dwells without. such is the
name that it gives form
to thought, to what had once
only been imagined. and now
you are both form
and thought, and your beauty

will be sung again and
again as your rivers flow
into infinity. O Cibao,
Jamaica, the Caribbees,
I utter your names, and they
take on the magic light, and
the sublime of your mountains

defines the text of all time.
here the Columbian world
is written of as another wonder.
what did not exist proliferates
in immortal print, and the
sublime of my inner harbors
gives rise to the beautiful bay.

II. To the Shores of Paradise

AT THE ALTAR OF ANOTHER VOYAGE

God, I come before you
again to ascertain
the reasons for my failure.
everywhere I search
there is no Word but hovels,

no elegant courts but
the poor and disenfranchised.
I seek the monastery, the
sepulcher of your Word, the
chalice wherein it radiates

its all-powerful light;
and all I find are shards
of gold. I come to you again
in the habit of a friar
to express my humility

and to ask for help.
I have taken up abode
under the roof of a priest
in order to be more
intimate with you through

an emissary. what more
can I do? a sign of Cathay
is all I ask: a meteor,
a phantom, the mystical
speech of the night.

I pray before you humbly,
admitting to my arrogance:
it is the vision that sears
through me, a python that
crushes me to drive on. . . .

165

dare I say I have
achieved much in a
few short years and all
because you first gave me
the object upon which all

other objects coalesce?
but now to go on
I need a sign: to stir
myself and others—others
who have grown tired

and doubtful. . . .
I will sing your praises,
Lord, as a devout son—
but reveal your text to me
in one eternal flash.

TO ACT WITHOUT SIGNS

no sign from heaven
or from earth, but
the python beats in me,
and I must drive on
into the realm without signs

until one emerges, or
be satisfied with the
pulsations of the serpent.
for we move now without
a manifestation, and all

our vigor courses through
the lean body of desire.
drive on, drive on men
into the lascivious Atlantic
South and West again

drive on, because you will
be dead if I catch you
idle! and I myself feel
a startling energy as if
I had been dead and come

back to life: the python
throbs in me like bolts
of killing lightning; and
I am awake. it is the universe
and me in a death grip,

and such life I feel now
tingles with the fever
of non-existence. here is my
border, cross it says death,
and I step gladly over

the margin; but only
to step back with the
renewed passion of the
passenger: electric thrills,
fire that burns the bone

with a power to kill.
drive on, I say, for
the python will wring your
neck for the joy of pain,
and a darkness will fall

over you to make you curse
you ever lived. drive on! . . .
and now we stand alone
in the macabre universe,
I and my other soul;

what will come of us
who fathom the depths of
solitude, who will write
our epitaphs if we die?
a strange feeling of awe

comes over me, as if a sign,
but no sign from heaven
but myself—the python
rises to my breath,
against the sky!

UNLOCK THE SIGN

vast sea, will you unlock
your sign? Atlantic,
will you answer my cries
that wake the whales
of your depths? if God

has abandoned me, will
you at least give form
to the mystery hovering
over your waves? blustery
winds that rock us across

the watery spaces, will
you blow something through
the stagnant sky, a sign
of marvelous Cathay?
I see an island emerge in

the infinite gray, the
world widens and widens:
is it a sign? I call it
Trinidad; for the Trinity
will perhaps bestow upon

us the gift of a signature.
and onward through the
Gulf of Paria, and onward.
is this Cathay? a mainland
that extends throughout the

East? yes, and the
fresh waters emptying here,
such splendor: the roots
of Paradise, the mouth of
the Ganges. a sign to be

sure of that Garden fountain
whose history many
have recorded. . . .
bliss—for in that moment
the spectral pearl rises from

the depths, a sudden
burst of icy light,
a magnificent gesture of
Paradise. who can challenge
me now that I am not

the future bearer of the Word?
it is here I must return
(for Hispaniola calls in
its grief). God bless the
depths—for they reflect the image.

III. Ode to Invention

to accept only on blind faith
the world as a given, a concept
already settled upon, a
concrete entity whose dimensions
have been recorded and passed
down; to accept the planet
as having an ancient history

stretching back to the prehistoric
caves, whose very history
presupposes a future; to accept
the earth as no more than a
sphere among other spheres
in interstellar space,
ruins the quality of living

for the curious; could be
said to be myth at work
as science, the darkness that
passes for the light. nothing
imagined is real unless it is
wholly imagined, not belief
in the passive corridors of the

mind but acute perception
of the as yet lived experience.
invention gives us the world
anew, changes the temperature
of the known in a moment's heat,
alters the terms of reality
upon which to understand what

had seemed unchangeable.
invention alters imagination
itself, for imagination will now
have to assume a changed position
in relationship to change.
how quickly the world vanishes
in the pendulum of invention's

clock; how remarkable it is
that shadow becomes light
and light again shadow.
and from where does
invention come? from the
throbbing fever of imagination
illumined by invention.

for now we are entering
the sea of our creation:
that flux of the blood in the
crashing waves. what a
marvelous tempest descends
upon us, altering the skies from
blue to red and the waves

from green to black; what joy
comes over us who had
been depressed by the wisdom
of the ages. in the suspension
of the rainbow in the closure
of the wracking winds, there
walks invention, clothed

like an angel, a psalm in
his voice for change. invent,
invent, cry out for the
dismemberment of the universe.
for only then the world will
spin into the ocean of destiny—
beyond the fissures of time.

IV. The Earth Closed Off

ON THE NATURE OF REBELLION

it is the mind at war
with the body and the
body at war with the
mind: such disenchantment
that leads to fractures

of the soul. here the
typical concert dissolves
in the cacaphonous thunder
of combat; and such bellowing
supersedes the greatest

wars of history.
I am standing on a
whirlpool of the earth.
all manner of order has
been thrown out like missiles

from the center. all
discourse breaks down into
phonetic grunts, disputatious
barks, a dyslexia of
the spirit. Hispaniola

will die if the rebellion
is not squashed; death
to invective, bury the
scoundrels who challenge
the order of the state.

python, well up in me
that we may crush the
detriments to our dynasty.
break their mouths
before they spew

the beauty of power:
ugly men who think
they can walk the same
earth as the brothers
Columbus: triumvirate

of the new Spain. wrestle,
my soul, to stay whole
against the rebellious
thunder; plant feet
on the dying backs

of these feeble Indians;
rescue the gold from
pillage by the lesser
order; retrieve the Columbian
legacy! it is to our text

that we owe the suppression
of disorder, the deconstruction
of invention: let our verbs
pray again for the cosmic
harmony of the pearl.

CHAINS AND METAPHYSICS

how was I to know
Bobadilla would find
the rebels hanging from
the gallows on his first
entrance to Santo Domingo—

like slaughtered sheep,
the cancer of the state?
to interpret this as disorder
is folly; it was done with all
intent of order and decency.

and that great opportunist
slavishly serving the King
and Queen for the gold and
the profit of fame! how could
the sovereigns deny me Paradise?

O God please intercede
in this crime against
your Word, in this
devastation of the miraculous
text whose spirit permeates

the world. in chains
I remain your humble
servant, reduced to the
lot of a beast. my heart
blasts out against

the despoilers of my
legacy! they who desire
only fame and wealth—
to steal the titles
of my discoveries.

no, I will not be free!
for the sovereigns have
ordered these chains and I
will bear them to Spain.
leave me alone with

the sea and its sublime
fidelity. I will sort
out my grief in solitude,
I will leave my fate
to the planet's movements.

I do not need your solace
whose silence implicates
you in all the acts
against me; who sully
my family's name,

the honor of the state.
God grant me pity
whose heart is weighed
down by chains,
whose wrists are sore

with such a metaphysical
pain. I am a beast
dispossessed
of his fields,
wandering this sea-earth

as prey. who will find
your Word now that
your adventurer is dead,
your angelic beast?
free me so that I may

voyage to the other side
of heaven—there where
the cool plain will wipe
my brow and the thunder
will throb no more.

V. Maria's Fourth Monologue

you begin to understand
that paradise exists within,
that our love will show
the green of eternal spring,
the fruit of miraculous trees.
but you continue your quest
for the outer paradise, nevertheless,

and the distance between
reality and fantasy will
grow, multiplying the disasters
of your adventures in the
other world. look into
yourself, Columbus, and attempt
to close the gap between the possible

and the infinite-improbable.
for in this terrible chasm
exists destruction. on the edge
of madness, you will fall into
that abyss preordained for the
arrogant, for prominent sinners,
an abyss not only of the soul

but of the mind, as it plummets
from layer to layer of morass
and excruciating pain. I have
heard each layer contains a phantom
of psychic illness: an agonizing
scream; an acute vertigo;
a suffocating weight;

a chiaroscuro of whirling
speed; scenes of torture;
utter and ineffable darkness—
and that the sinners must repeat
their names at every layer
to confirm their guilt, to act out
the life of sin in its bloody

particulars. Columbus, I
warn you to sail away from
irreality, to float in the world
of the waters as they exist;
for beyond your mind is the
whole destiny of a race, and I see
nothing but devastation ahead.

there is hardly time to mend that gaping
wound—the slaughter, the butchered
hands, the suicides, the starvation
of spirit and body, the certain
genocide—but you must try.
I beseech you to come to your senses
before the very cosmos turns

against you, and our love
is forever lost. for Columbus,
though I have loved you for your
visionary groping, your restless
imagination, your nervous aspirations,
these all will die in the fantasies
of your cargo beyond our shores.

Book Five

THE FOURTH VOYAGE

I. Hymn to the Terrestrial Paradise

such fresh water could
not mean other than
Paradise: the water of Eden's
well: from here the Ganges,
the Nile, the Tigris, and
the Euphrates all originate—
it is that source

of which the texts of many
authors speak, of which
the central text speaks
with reverence. here
in Paria I have found the mouth
of the Ganges and the origin
of our testament to the world;

here I have located the
Garden where our ancestors
roamed without fear of ridicule;
here I have discovered
the very origins of innocence.
ah, to that time when nakedness
was as natural as

bird song, when the outer
and the inner corresponded
as if one, without the
intervention of consciousness.
such fertility of human
and nature uncorrupted by
abstractions, treatises on destiny,

theories of the Negative!
O golden time . . .
but that magic has been
lost and for the better
in the end—because nature
rears its violent head, O
python crushing the very throat

of innocence, O beauty of
the death we have inherited,
O stealthy, corrupt man
who boldly marks the text
of the future. yet it is here
the Word may be found.
terrestrial Paradise, here

where I can unleash
the virile energy of God's
text; the holocaust of the
Word; the medicine of Scripture.
O earthly Paradise,
I seek the sepulcher
beneath your olive trees . . .

the belly of the monastery.
here, to go beyond
historical fame, to be
redeemed in God's eyes.
for all the texts of the past
have led to this, this moment
of the pearl in its icy light.

and I myself have entered
this light, and all my
ships have entered this
light, and the Atlantic
has entered this light
as well. we are all flowing
to Paradise.

for this light of the
ultimate cosmos, the Word
of the light of the ultimate
cosmos, was ready to explode
upon the world, and when I came
with my ships to see,
then it arose.

II. Trials and Persecutions

THE SEA AS ORIGIN

I have suffered the bloody
chains of the mind for
four years and am back
on the road of the sea,
there to find the Paradise

of that other world
where all things flow.
the sea seduces in its
charms, calls out its chants
even to one as old and tired

as myself. the very silver
seems to draw me down.
the waves in their laving
music hypnotize. white sails
stretched taut in the wind

transport me. I am
mesmerized by the clouds.
nothing is good unless I
voyage, nothing makes sense.
the mind struggles for

coherence, but it wanders
without the thrust of the
prow, the dashing foam
of a rough sea, the slithering
gulls that make magic

out of air. nothing makes
sense. not even the land
without the sea in my
view. it is the frame
within which all other things

exist: a vector of consciousness,
a vortex that gathers up
all life and death, the
ultimate crystal of my life.
here I began and here I

will end. here I have
struggled, here I transcend.
counting the waves, I have
touched infinity; watching
the sands, I have embraced

the eternal. the sea is
my origin—and there I
would like to be buried.
within its flow,
in the tow of its waves,

I would sink, forever
separate from the stress
of earth. there I would
float and rest
among its bones.

REPULSED

on the order of the
sovereigns I was not to
touch at Santo Domingo.
such humiliation I could
bear but once;

yet to be repulsed again
in the throes of a storm
with my provisions low
was beneath the dignity
of my office. swine Ovando,

who has leapt to power
on the wings of my discoveries!
any man of civil bent
would help another in the
eye of so dark a storm,

and we flying the same
colors, worshiping the
same God! what more
do they want of me who
have suffered such indecencies,

such insults to my name,
my notion of Eden, salvation,
and the Word? for there is gold
to be found in that other
world; and even that

they mock. the fools!
I will show them with
my fist shaking the
golden Word, immaculate
birth of a new civilization!

I will show them the
center of the hidden
cosmos, the plenitude of
wealth in our father's
text, and gold

mounting to heaven.
I may be old and tired,
but I have enough wrath
left in me to unbury
the absolute.

God, help me through
this storm as I suffer
the gloom of nature and
humanity. tempest in
my heart, rejection

by imbeciles, repulsed
because I bear the truth.
dark storm, pour your
bitter rains upon their heads,
but have mercy on mine.

VERAGUA AND DESTINY

the storm is dead in me
except for the hunger of
the Word. I ask God
after the morning prayer
about our prospects;

he descends on the deck
in full robes. he compares
me to Moses, to David;
he urges that I go on
believing in myself and

the monarchs. he says that
prospects lie in the power
of belief, and that our
dialectic of curse
and bestowal will persist.

is it here in Veragua?
no, not here in Veragua,
but such mountains of
gold, auriferous
dream . . .

it is here beyond Cibao
where our fortune will
be found . . . O monarchs,
such altars will be built
of the material sublime!

and from here, only
ten days separate us from
the Ganges and
the green of Eden. it is here
we will master the human

race; it is here, save it from
self-destruction. . . .
Lord, I am your voyager,
your hermeneutist of the seas:
my lips recite your Word.

III. Ode to Perseverance

when some stop for too
much pain against the
breastbone of spirit, I
continue. walking in circles,
I find the way. bone tired,
I rest but a minute in order
to resume the race of the waters.

perseverance, my consort,
the quality of habit,
giving shape to the quest,
perspective to vision,
without which we would be
defeated and home in the arms
of love. you offer a construct

for the longing temperament,
a logarithm of signs,
a coefficient in a world of
variance. when I tremble
in the heart of this vision,
I turn to you as the solid form
of depth, catalyst without

movement, object through
which the objective is met.
torn literally to shreds
with doubt, I know my mind
will not be long at this
ruptured doubleness, for
you perseverance will revive the

single purpose of the hunt.
in the black sky of spirit
and the white ether of all
thought, when death seems a
sweet alternative to aching joints
and blinding eyes and recurrent
nightmares of lynxes and

venomous snakes, I can
rely on your form to appear
out of the shimmering black,
a tether to my madness—
which swells from an explosive
caldron, a lava of all ills.
there you are, perseverance, in the dark. . . .

history and myth are
filled with figures of
perseverance: dissidents,
architects of destiny, rebels of
the word. Sisyphus for one,
whose rock signified shame,
in the end achieved heroism.

such fortitude in the endless
succession of tasks: to shove
stone; then defeat; and once more
to repeat the ritual: to accept
humiliation from the gods,
and then spit back at them—
the acceptance of the rock

in his heart and the
lifting of the weight once
again. a punishment, to be
sure, but transformed into
an act of valor. . . . Christ
lifted his cross in much
the same way—once, on

the historical stage, but
countless times in our lives—
yet with the added trauma
of lacerations and insults,
curses from the pagans,
stones to his Word and flesh;
and that final drama

of nailed hands bleeding
forever and forever onto
the eye of memory. whoever
refuses to see this blood
refuses the power of his own
death, the everlasting
testament, the driving ethos

of perseverance. the world soul
is sustained in the dying of
Christ on his cross, in the
arms of his mother.
and in the rock of Sisyphus,
the world soul also takes fire—
though the rock rises slowly

to the apex of the hill
only to fall into an abyss.
what magic in the image of the one
smitten to lift himself again, as
the other lifted himself into
the home of the eternal patriarch.
so many turns, so many turns . . .

and perseverance, I call
on you once more to lift me up—
but only in the act of lifting
myself—for there are countless
rocks to be pushed uphill:
up to his beautiful head,
bent to the heavens.

IV. Marooned

TO THE FACE OF GOD

ships down, pumps
working but useless
after so many leaks
and brutal weather.
lucky to find the shores

of Jamaica. here now
nearly a year and
every day I ask is this the
final test? has God
put me to the rack

in order to shake me
out for the ultimate
act, or to destroy me? with
my bones aching from the
wind and rain and my eyes

ready to close out the
light, I am in awe to be
still alive; but every day
I rage against a fate
that knocks me

from the quest, and
every day I beat my breast
against the darkening
skies. what do you want,
Lord, of your acolyte,

who has waged war
against inclement weather
and a warlike peoples,
against a mutinous crew
who want nothing more

than the comforts of
Spain? I gash my flesh
in order to close the circle
between us, but you as
much as laugh in my face.

what comfort do you take
in my exile, my profound
solitude? on this island
I have confronted despair
in its purest state and

have probed the deepest
darkness, and all you do
is blow us squalls, crack
your whip of lightning, and
stir the passions of the Indians

against us. . . .
can I withstand the hour
when the head returns
to the ground? Maria,
walk with me on the

burning path of the grave;
kiss my forehead that
thumps with sin's pain. . . .
you have no right, God,
to steal my sanity—

the mind that sought
your Word! save me
before I blaspheme your
sacraments: steer your lions
of wrath into the bay.

I can curse
as soon as love, can
strike back the skies that
smite me down, heave my sword
unto the moon, scourge

the innocent baptized . . .
head, spin out this
dreary vertigo; God
save me from the vortex . . .
I spend the night in a

hypnagogic void under
the skies. there the python
spells power in
red flame, slithering
into my dream.

what can I know of the
future stranded on this
wasteland, an island unto
myself; what remedies
exist in his scheme?

THE PYTHON

roll in your fire,
vengeful flame, roll
in the luminous sin of
evil and decay, roll
down time from your pyre

in the firmament, roll
on the seas splendid for
your light, on the shoals
red in the wake of your
almighty tail, and the

carcasses left aflame
in your sweet apocalypse.
roll to me over the corpses
of my crew who sleep,
paint their dreams red

with flame, cover the
island with your incandescent
fire, bellow conflagration.
O roll to me
who stares at death

with the persecuted face of
a god . . . roll in your fire
up to me, swaddle my
feet with flame, torch
all my clothes and let

them burn that I may
live. lave my body
with your waves of smoke,
curl your music up
my spine, O rapturous

flame make all my
cells sing in lascivious
sin. roll up to me, roll
around my entire frame,
roll the *lux* of your power

around the shadows
of my tendons, the dark
lineage of my muscles.
roll to me who call your
name. O up, up—up

the chest, over the entire
torso, wake to me who
sleeps with death, roll
to me who longs for
vengeance. at the

midnight hour, wrap
your flame around
my head that it may
exorcise the pain, O wrap
and turn your fires

into the cavities of my
eyes. roll and fan . . .
but stop, stop, stop there
at the neck where the air,
at the neck where the air . . .

O crushing power,
crushing power. God
my savior, crushing power.
air, I need air, crushing
power . . . O electrode

whose ray pours its
charge into my throat . . .
air, I need air!
this is not Cathay,
this is not Cathay.

V. Maria's Fifth Monologue

my wounded Columbus,
you have reached the state
of madness I predicted
and will have to suffer
the full strength of the serpent's
virile grip: the force your own
sick rootedness gave life to.

there is no escaping the
crush of the python, as he
strangles you with the hatred
of essential nature, a hatred
we attach to it in our conscious
needs. he will seem to break
your nape before life flows

again in its troubled frenzy,
pulsating in its deepest
necessity. you will have
learned little from this love
of death except to live.
the next time we kiss it will be
as a woman anguished by

passion and a man embarking
on the priesthood. to deny
all physical joy because of such
consuming physical pain
is to deny our compact with the
earth. Columbus, returning
to your God with such severity

will only lead in the end
to an abstinence of spirit, a
deepening stress against the
life force, even the world soul.
no account of sins will absolve
you from the verdict of the soul's
jury, or revive the many

of the Other, the many, many
who were swept down by the
python's glazed eye of destruction.
only our marriage, whose house
reveals the fissures of our love,
can redeem you, and only
love (I whisper the word for

it stings my lips) can
retrace your longings to their
vital source. having botched
the outer quest (but with some
immanent beauties and unconscious
marvels) you must map the
inner world with more discretion.

your recognition that your
Other World and Cathay are
not coterminous already
suggests a new geography for
your soul. be guided by that
recognition, for therein lies
a powerful constituent of the real,

a real you have evaded
in your masculine pursuit
of the ideal. but to be guided
now by the mythography of false
belief will distort the geography
once again, will drive your soul
in a storm to the wrong shores.

only love, even in its
fragile form, will pull up
sails for you on the cordage
of grace and mercy, will
beckon in its sweet rondure,
will guide you on the right seas
to the home of the perfect

imperfection. there you will
hear the music of the nightingale,
or of the softly lapping waves,
some echo of a previous life
to which you now give form.
these are the shores, the right shores,
of the beautiful, blue night.

Book Six

RETIREMENT I

I. Hymn to An Other World

across the subtle seas
I found Cathay, and lived
the deceit as if the truth,
because all my life
depended on it—because
the world was ripe for such
a lie. a remarkable lie,

in fact, but only made
more radiant by the brutal
snake, the lock that closed
the air on all that vision.
yet subtle as the seas
and the python's slithery
power, an other world emerged

in the vacuum. let me
sing a hymn to it now
as it takes its place on the
maps of all the imaginers.
O how the world has grown!
what a gem posterity
will wear of the new earth,

a necklace of the shores
that stretch from island
to terra firma: blue coast
of the sun-drenched continent.
an other world to us because
there was no other world;
an other world than the one

we now inhabit. what
can we learn from this?
not only what it bears but
the inborn truth of ourselves
as well. for we are newly
defined, an other world ourselves,
a miracle in the mirror

of our being. this is worthy
of a name, but a name eludes
me now: two other worlds
hidden from view through
centuries of shadow and
weakening wills.
yet I stand on the threshold

between these worlds
and my stomach sickens
at the thought of evil, ruinous
snake of my body, poisonous
vision. . . . Lord, help your passenger;
lead me onto the path of redemption,
the abstaining spirit of joy and light.

II. The Seven Deadly Sins, Part I

PRELUDE

having survived the grip
of the python in Jamaica
in a year of utter waste
and exhaustion, solitude
and morass, I sailed

through the love of
a few to Santo Domingo,
where the ocean currents
one last time swept me
up. all voyages done,

and only political tempests
to navigate, here in Spain
I make an account of
my soul on its journeys in
those years. I have vowed

a fortnight of silence,
so as to be closer to my
breath, and to that of God.
my breath is the breath
of the near dead who have

suffered a violent aggression.
now I must meditate
to calm the tiger
that rips my entrails;
now travel to

an inner space away from
the torrents. and there
at the numinous center
I can once again live
the storm of my history.

for all my sins and
errors will rise with the
hull of the shipwreck; in
the meditative dream, my
soul will set its sights.

PRIDE

from my first conjuring
of the Western experiment
I suffered pride. such
fantasy, I then called
vision, evolving from

the grandiose but the
melancholic also. what
expansion of the ego in
order to overcome the
pain of uncertainty!

what a fabrication of
the truth in order to dare
the seas! it was pride when
I said no one else had thought
of this, this route to the

golden East—except
Toscanelli, of course.
but no one had dared
the Atlantic in its breadth—
and such a plan! it was pride

when I imposed myself on the Other,
for how could these innocents
know anything of the world?
this is the world,
I insisted, this is its God.

bow down to his hallowed feet.
but as they bowed, I crushed
them, wrapped my python
around their necks . . .
O pride where have you led me?:

such a labyrinth from
which I may never emerge.
so many turns and never
a candle, so many contortions
of the soul. when will you lift

your weight? . . . forgive me this
sin, Lord, that I may ascend
to your kingdom;
for there the humble sing
glorias of their great luck.

WRATH

I have destroyed
the tree of life with
my wrath; for even in
my early appeals before the
courts of Europe,

I secretly blasphemed
the monarchs on rejection.
behind their backs
I spat on their image,
ridiculed their intelligence,

wished them to hell.
and even before that
I disparaged my family
for their provincial tastes.
and on my first voyage,

with greatness before me
in the curves of wave and sky,
I cursed my men with a
venom I had never before
experienced. for how could

they deny me fame?
and on my second voyage
when the Other became not
a resident of paradise
as much as a potential enemy

in my mind, my rage
shot out like thunderbolts
against them . . . but
I cannot withstand a review
of these barbarities,

dull in intensity—
the brutal taxation, the
hand chopping—nightmares,
crimes against humanity!
pestilence and disease.

slap me down, God,
with the prongs of your own
wrath—you who have
suffered my verbal
scourges—for I

am not worthy of
your kingdom unless I
suffer purgatorial damnation.
slap me down,
I who have lived by wrath.

SLOTH

there is little sloth
in my history except
the sloth of the mind.
for how could I not
overcome through reason

and intellection the
sloppiness of my imagination?
how could I not,
when studying the Western
question, defeat

the stubborn need in me
to search, the irreal
and the grandiose with
the mathematics of the mind?
or even allowing for

that first step across
the Ocean Sea, why did
I not reevaluate
my position on Cathay
after so much evidence,

after the other world
had presented in its
flora and fauna, in its
racial character, all
signs of an entirely

different continent?
for now as I have come
to that recognition, sloth
rears its ugly head—
so much needless death,

so much needless death.
God, forgive me for this
sin of sloth, for I will
try to exercise my mind
like a laborer in the fields,

and follow your sun
with virtue and vitality.
here, in silence,
I screw my mind to your
Word with working sweat.

ENVY

envy has driven me
to quest, to conquest,
to total destruction; even
to romantic dispute.
for in envy lurks

a force of utter denial:
denial of oneself, denial
of the other. . . . in those
early yearnings for
exploration, for example,

I sat with my arms crossed
waiting for a decision:
impatient, perturbed,
all the time envious
of Henry the Navigator

for his capacity to
envision and to enact.
I looked on as he
commissioned ships to
Africa and poked daggers

in his heart out of envy;
I beat my chest out of
a tremendous desire to
move, to explore,
to discover: I was like

a caged animal who,
failing to elude his
pursuer, paces the narrowing
world of his prison.
where could I go for solace?

to Maria? even she I
envied for her sure-
footedness, her composure,
her self-confidence, her
love of the real. till

this day we argue with
such a passion over the
real and the visionary,
the earth-view and the
sea-view, the powers

of love and the powers
of the utter beyond.
I have disturbed our love
with my insistence on
the boundless quest,

envying those borders
that persist as the
demographics of the heart.
and envy is limitless;
like avarice it knows

no end. only destruction
satisfies the passion
for an instant, and once
again it rules the heart.
so I destroyed the Other

out of the need to stop
the pangs of envy and
because I envied them
as well: their paradise,
their communal forms,

their love of the earth
and each other. and so
it is now as I meditate
in utter silence, that envy
will not stay quiet:

a raucous ringing in
my ears, the wave-throbs
of my heart. God, have
mercy on your worshiper
who is overcome by the

noise of envy, by
the perpetual motion of
its sickness. I want quiet,
I want quiet, I want quiet.
give me the silence unto death.

III. Ode to Humility

pride is the death of us
who hope to be good Christians,
for Christ set the example
with his humble heroism.
turning water into wine,
reviving the dead, did not
embolden him with pride,

inflate the ego of his godly
self. Christ stood a god
without the need of office,
the pretensions of godhood,
the golden crown of a head
of state. he was all
humility even as he swayed

the masses. for Christian
love depends so much on
the surrender of self, the
subordination of worldly possessions
to spirit, the valorization of our
connections to other human beings,
compassion—that Christ knew

implicitly he must sacrifice
all the powers of his godly
status, in order to preach the
Word, spread the text of the
new order over the world.
and it was his character to
do so, in any event, for no

pride ruled the man as in my
own case. humility, I call on
you now as one who has violated
the code of meekness, subservience,
and service to a higher destiny.
for I have lived my life
according to the destinies of

self and power, embraced
the worldly, cursed God in my
failure to find his Word, became
so full of the glories of the here
and beyond I myself became a
god. humility, you are the
path upon which we must trod

in order to find our road
to heaven. it is God who
has given us the gift of
breath, and it is to him
we owe our existence—
yet we boast as if there
were no progenitor of our

words and deeds.
humility, I read your
text with the studiousness
of an acolyte, a religious
dreamer . . . with Christ
I walk the path
of resurrection's light.

IV. The Seven Deadly Sins, Part II

AVARICE

for the love of gold
I have killed, for the
love of gold I have
turned nature into
a work camp, for the

love of gold I have
committed the sin of avarice—
an insatiable sin of desire,
a sin inhabiting a cancerous
body, and never ending

until the body can covet
no more. O gold, that
I have worshiped
with the yearnings of a
zealot, yellow vision

of sun, God-bestowing
light, chimerical wonder,
and yet so real in
your capacity to build
and buy, translatable

matter of the earth.
gold, I have worn your
dust in my hair, your
metal in the retinas
of my eyes—for all my

vision was gold and
the magnificent future
was gold in its roads.
and for gold I have walked
the decks of my mystical

body, for gold I have
slept little of the
sleep of men, for gold
I have enslaved, for
gold I have butchered

those I thought unresourceful—
for gold I have forced some
to suicide. beautiful gold,
for this I have sinned
and will be damned . . .

unless God turns my
head forever from the
yellow bliss that
even now seduces.
longings for gold,

longings. . . .
O Lord, take my hand
into the forest of peace
and light, where these
longings will tempt no more.

GLUTTONY

I have never myself
been gluttonous within
our cultural code,
being too restless for
food of any quantity,

too nervous in the quest—
a quest that demanded
every bit of my hunger.
but I have never discouraged
my men from fulfilling

their bestial appetites,
their corporal lusts,
barely satiable and
disproportionate
next to the Indians.

for a Spaniard could
consume in one day what
an Indian family would eat
in a month. only now do I
see the consequences

of such consumption:
a nature raped cold,
ravaged by desires to
indulge—beyond all
need of sustenance,

beyond the need of
maintenance of our human
acts. for we pillaged the
body of the world in order
to profit our own. God,

forgive me this sin of my
weak will, the impoverishment
of my authority, for I
allowed your earth to be
farmed beyond all reason,

your animals to be slaughtered
beyond reasonable need,
all degree of moderation
abused by the beasts
of our herd. God,

I once more bow before
your altar, taking a vow
of moderation in all forms,
for the gluttonous will die
of their own consumptive stench.

LECHERY

my love of women
is great, but I cannot
confess to any lecherous
behavior in my life;
for Maria has been so

prominent, and for so
many decades. she is
love and sex in the
one body of marriage, a
splendid light of passion

and intellect. yet, Lord,
I know I have lusted
in my dreams after the
women of the other world,
have fondled their breasts,

sought intercourse
underwater. their bronze
nudity all shimmering by
day, cloaked in my dark
arms by night: pale dreams

of eros, exultations
of wished-for love.
but the abstract was
always so immense a
distillation and my

passionate needs fed off
the quest. and of course
Maria was there in the
shadow of eros,
awaiting fulfillment,

scorning whatever
indiscretion might be
latent in the fantastic.
at least, Lord, my vow of
fidelity held firm.

but not for my men
who raped at will and
with such consuming force . . .
blight of their testament,
my weakness to govern . . .

empire! empire!
the mark of the masculine
upon the indigenous:
the impersonal dynamo
unearthing, disrupting,

consuming, distorting,
mangling, and marring
the germ and the source.
mea culpa, mea culpa,
mea maxima culpa. . . .

and here I will remain,
Lord, in the silence of time,
awaiting your decree—
will I survive, or drift
forever from your light?

CODA: THE PYTHON II

scream out, for the
python moves across
the naked floor, into
the shaft of light of
dawn—in a clarity

of line unusual for
the mammoth creature.
scream out, for the
noise may break the
stamina of his will.

deep in the memory
the ego falls, to find
the root of the flesh's
response, when fear stirs
the bones and blood

rushes into the waiting
brain; and blood rushes
like rain about to end
its cyclic time. scream out,
for inches move into feet

and the sliding light
dares death with its
death-like dance.
pulsations of the whole
corporal legend, the body

thumping in its history—
phenomena appear before
the sleeping eye. what
can I do to stop
the stopping flow, how

to rid the fever of
its trance? the python
acts because it must,
according to its nature,
it knows no deliberation

before eternity. and so
it moves unto my neck
with the sure beauty
of its forceful purpose:
consciously unconscious,

a hesitation only in the
assumption of a posture:
a proper figure for pain.
and I wonder, in this grip
of the bracing claim,

was there a prefiguration
of this, somewhere in that
dark prehistory of my name,
somewhere before I even knew
to know; and to touch

that source would end
this vengeful grip,
this unrelieving pressure
on my life pulse? scream
out, for the python

moves to suck all
life from your bleeding
neck . . . I want air,
I said air, give me air,
I want . . . air!

V. Maria's Sixth Monologue

and so the python came
again unto your neck,
and so the python came
once more to steal your air.
O, if only you had listened
to my warnings before—and
now you suffer incredible pain.

but like death that sharpens
our will to live, the pain
unleashes your monstrous
energies, purges you of that
disease wallowing in every
ventricle of your history.
you will be free of it for good.

do not turn back, my dear
Columbus, to those life-
denying constraints of a
religious vow, for the python
will always break the walls of
your inner monastery. he knows
better the deeper urges of your

life, the dark light of
everything you have revealed
to the world. but his sickly
grip will ultimately end your
quest, and what is your life
except a quest, and what are our
lives except that question that

remains forever unanswered,
a love in the process of getting
to know its very processes?
I told you our love was about
to die, but it can live again
if you embrace love—and redemption
will come only on condition

you surrender the otherworldly
pursuit of the answer. here we
are again confronting ourselves
across the threshold of real
and irreal, and only the real
can soothe the deep tremors of
the after shock. as you turn now

to art as salvation, remember that
no creation endures without love:
love of the artist and the art lover
in league with a form that seals
their love across the nights of
centuries, across the oceans of
calm and storm: form translatable

from the stamen of historical
flame. for it is the drive
of love in its temporal moment
that beats out the form in
its conscious mold, like sex
beating life into the human body,
like sex breathing its signature

across chaos and chasm.
in your journey now to Oceania,
remember these thoughts for
good art will come from them,
and redemption will follow. in
the powerful nexus between you and
the other world, remember our love:

herein is the real source of all
art; for life folds and folds again
in the waves of its blood.
for there is no end to its hunger,
and there is no end to its thirst.
and we will be forever walking
the world in the shoes of Mercury.

Book Seven

RETIREMENT II

I. Hymn to Oceania

released from the land
and the lock of his tail
I sailed on the patient sea,
swearing off all things human,
God's law, and my way in
the world . . .
I floated here,

as on vaporous water, to find
a new view. Oceania,
island of my prehistory, blue
haven, rugged shore,
mountainous land. O sea-earth
where memory is unleashed.
the future will ignite

in your cleavage of stone;
and I will whirl up in your
sky-radiance. Oceania,
I come to you to strip off
my old self—now in its
desiccation ready to be peeled
away; in your sublime

mountains to build a new self
forged from the rhythms of
your waves; in your flowers
to put new urgency in my sensory
life. for I was dead in Spain
and the crowds of hero-worshipers
and detractors penetrated

the little peace left me.
here I will find my way
without God—in the caves
of the interior; will raise
questions I could never raise
before; will free my spirit
from its Christian cage.

for within its law I could
never see the light of
Grecian purity, objective truth,
the blue resonance of shore and
sky. yet the dark must come
with the light—a tragic
lucidity. what can you give

me of the night, Oceania,
that it may not be filled
with the terror of constraint,
the diabolic portents of hell,
the demons who inhabit
our forests and mountains?
poetry wells up in me like

a tidal wave, a shock to
the old system of the transcendent.
here there seems to be
a new way to breathe into the
beyond-us. yet so late an art,
at the threshold of my end.
what to do? how to begin?

I meditate in the blue,
begin to observe forms,
resist the call of the sea
into the folds of death . . .
wait for me, wait for me,
for the text rises ever so
gently out of silence.

II. Meditations, Part I

FAREWELL TO GOD

for too many years
the dialectic between us
consumed my utter
attention, like a great
ocean of tremorous storm.

I grew to live with it
as a married man in
an unhappy marriage
might begin to await
the bitter words and

killing stares of the
exciting drama of the
daily. for my life
with you was theater
and I was the actor

born to fluctuate
with the changing scripts.
and there you stood
unchanging in your
impenetrable heights,

a father enjoying
the failures of his son.
I grow now toward freedom,
taking responsibility
for my sins and errors

but without the paternal
code, the rigid forms
we have made of your
Word. and so it is I
have come to this in part

because of that Word
and its illusiveness,
I foundering on the ocean
of my quest without as much
as a sign from you

of its whereabouts.
so on the winds of the world
I flew, a lost soul in
sea-space, my eyes glazed
over with the power

implicit in my being
confidant to the Lord God.
but beyond our private
dialectic, I have realized
my sins and errors

are rooted in our
Christian ethos.
for your Church,
Lord, has slaughtered
millions in your name.

Christ is dead on the
sword of our bloody
revenges, our imperial
drives, our lust to
master body and soul. . . .

and here I have come
to confess all, but without
the inflictions of our holy rite.
for if I now seek redemption,
it will not be with

the damnation of the soul,
but of the flesh—
in ways in which its text
will burn a scar into
a future of the good.

ARS POETICA I

traveling on the outer seas
of the world, in the
trade winds, in black
squalls enveloping
our entire destinies,

I saw the beauty of
the quest; here I was
champion of my fate,
and here I made contact
with the beyond-us.

for those days of blue
or sudden black and
the nights decorated
with constellations—
intimacy and the immensity

of the ocean space and
the whole globe surrounding
us—took my breath
from its normal rhythms
into the rapturous

heart pulse of the
cosmos. on the porch
of my floating house
I was driven up into
that silent drama,

the brilliant sonority
of the sky. what could
be wrong with a world
that played such
splendid music?

it was the poetry of
outer forms: curvatures
of cloud and arches of
sky, and music in the
motion of the firmament.

there was my text
inscribed on a sea of
changes: blue oasis of
the illimitable, turbulent
tides leaping over the stern;

and then beneath in that
ineluctable depth, the
poetry spoke as from death:
the dark bliss of the
mystical, where our eyes

were drawn to the strange
light. and so it was
in the sublime universe
poetry throbbed in
the nature of things:

the sea was my epic,
my natural métier,
where all joys and all
troubles formed a
symphonic poem.

the land ruined that
poem, tore into its
harmonies like a shark
a mummified whale.
the delicious cosmos

became a political
imbroglio. I stood in
the cracks of the poem
hoping to reconstruct it,
but it collapsed in a heap

of a discordant nightmare.
there is beauty in that
other world, nevertheless,
and a hope for the millenium,
and the fractures sparkle

with incorrigible vigor.
here the poem must be
made again: the traumas
of space-time, the tragedy
of culture and epoch.

here I must begin to
recreate, with words on
the page, to overcome
the cosmic poem
of my first search.

here I must make
a poem where language
reorders the world . . .
and now I must meditate
to find it.

ARS POETICA II

and so, I might ask,
why poetry for my
life story? would prose
not be better suited
for the full particulars,

the minute details of
the tragedy? the sun
as much as answers in
its burst of light after
a day of steel clouds.

poetry for the sudden
light it is capable of. . . .
unveil yourself, my poem,
unto the future unborn,
prophesy. but speak

historically as well,
for no art can live
only for the future.
speak of the joys and
traumas, the pain and

fever; speak as the
keel of the spirit, the
body in its hungers,
the heart that repels
its silence. . . .

but in this space of blue
light, an anarchy of
solitude descends. the poem is
at the mouth where the mind
stands . . . let me read.

ARS POETICA III

it will be a tragic poem,
that I know, for it will
relate of the fall of the
hero and that other world
of his discovery. this

is the story, as I know
it, the content of the
form that remains
concealed. and it is in
tragedy that I must

find the source of the
narrative, for tragedy
speaks with the greatness
of revelation and descent,
moves us to grief

who would otherwise be
cold. it leaves us
upon an abyss, into
which we too would
fall but for the suggestion

it gives to reconstruct.
such an unresolved
image of the world
vacated by the hero,
such fractures at the center.

so we are invited to
imagine a future, in
our great pity to
rebuild the city of
posterity. the king is dead,

will his kingdom be
dead as well? that we
must take upon ourselves
as if bearers at his funeral:
it cannot be otherwise . . .

and this is my funeral
as well, where drama is
the recognition of that other
world. but where do I begin . . .
and how do I see?

III. Ode to Prophecy

when we awake, after
long sleep, we see as through
a cloud, the blur of all
objects, unfamiliar in their
familiarity by daylight,
but made more unfamiliar
in this haze of first light.

after many dreams, this haze
is heavier still: the room
is entirely foreign to us, as if
a room in another house, another
city. it is with startling
wonder that we see the objects
for themselves and are grateful

for the familiarity once again.
ah yes, this is the room of
my many lives, here I belong.
and so sight becomes an
adventure, a gift of the gods,
a voyage along the arteries
of perception.

I am a scientist of sight;
I have made a point of
looking: the very relatedness
of my eyes, all objects,
the Ocean Sea of the world.
the present stands there in
its flickering and superabundance.

the past is something else again:
with no eyes to rely upon,
it is the inner eye we must go
to then—connected to the
outer eye in the way to look,
and the outer eye of the past
in what it looked upon.

like the waking eye, there
is always the cloud to look
through; like the outer,
the inner must be exercised—
for the memory goes flat
without use. . . .
I make a point of

remembering; for to forget
destroys our racial
history. though the memory
was always a whale
roaming the sea of the mind,
it came second
to the next adventure.

but of the future, I have
had no experience whatsoever. . . .
O prophecy, give unto my eyes
the light of presentiment;
my mind the wonder of forevision;
my voice the articulate speech
of the foreteller.

in my silence and
stillness, it is you
I summon as muse.
O prophecy, help me to heal
the tragic wound: take me
to your workshop in the sky
and train me to see the years.

IV. Meditations, Part II

LUNAR SUN/SOLAR MOON

love rises in the face
of Maria, moon glow
of the rigorous spirit.
dwell in the house of
love before catastrophe

befalls you. such prophecy
I take with me over
the morning island.
walking, I find some
rhythms of the poem

that awaits. these are
the conditions of my
exile from the social
order. here I must
meditate despite my

restlessness for the poem.
here I must listen
and walk into the
interior spaces of the island.
I record my dreams

faithfully and take
notes on the terrain.
daily letters to Maria
sustain my love for
her; I insist on no

news of the social order.
I have never been happier—
except with her—yet I
have never worked so hard,
with a kind of torturous sweat.

dwell in the house of
love before catastrophe
befalls you. love is the
foundation of all art.
I search the mountains,

then the caves, caress
the river streams. track
the circumference of the
shoreline. love feeds art
the milk of generations.

such are the principles
I take with me over
the morning island.
luminous ball of sun
awaking the earth.

THE AUSTERE LIGHT OF POSSIBILITY

drafts, fragments,
false starts, lines
truncated midway.
abandon the text, abandon
the text, it is hopeless.

how could I be so
foolish as to think
I could master so difficult
an art? with no training,
no education, there was

little chance. and yet
I have come to this island
on a calling; and my story
seeps out at every pore
of my being. poetry

demands something
of my inner world that
has remained till this
point silently invisible,
a secret place to which

I need a code—an inner
sanctum where the
consciousness can barely
probe. love waits in the
light of the porthole,

but the darkness remains
an invisible script
on fine vellum. so tell me,
Maria, would it be better
that the project of love

go unwritten? and so
day passes to night
and night to day,
and as the heron lingers
for fish I linger for words.

abandon the text, abandon
the text, it is hopeless.
words crowd together
and barely let me sleep,
become nightmarish daggers

ripping my heart.
what do I need of this,
I whose last breath sings
at the sea? abandon the text . . .
and the story of my life?

but I seek comfort in the
heron's patience. wading
for hours on end, he seems
content to ponder water:
it will bring him grace,

he knows, in the end.
time stands with us
in its perpetual motion—
then falls away.
I look to the sea for

the first rhythm, the silent
music. there is no word
but an austere light; no word
but the faintest beam.
he soars.

V. Maria's Seventh Monologue

across the seas I observe
your face in the clarity
of its anguish. struggle,
struggle, for you are
approaching the illumination
of your life; for the imagination
can see with such a distance

invisible to us in our daily
minds. let it emerge out of
the buried atria of your heart.
let it emerge from the house
of love where it dwells with us
in silent anticipation. and there
is our love also, wading

on the stream of your vision:
it will survive only if you
dare to see. now on the
threshold of austerity, it appears
you have found the path of
your art: such form will come
of it if you awake to its tones

and rhythms. but this is all
exterior matter, I fear
Columbus, and you have so
much more work to do to
unblock that passion
sleeping at the heart of form.
your hope is in the anguish,

for to flee from it will
only upset the gathering force
of art. there is the pain
of all your life throbbing
in your brain: feel it as if it
were taking life from you;
observe it as one would the

movements of the stars. take
it to its bloody extreme
in macabre scenes of torture;
measure it as you would
the size of the earth. but do not
avoid the intensity of those throbs
or dismiss their seismic regularity.

now you are about to embark
on uncharted seas, seas of
green moss and mist, white
radiance of waves unbounded.
this is the bliss of love we can
again render in the unleashing
of your imagination; this is

the vessel of our future in
the architecture of form.
avert those waves and the
poem will forever remain
mute, deaf to life and love,
to art in its gradations
on the peaks of the sea. . . .

turn inward and further inward,
navigate those seas of the inner
eye—through waste and sludge,
through tempest, through treacherous
formations of the leviathan, through
lashes of the serpent long as your
ship; down, down, sail

under the mad sea and be done.
and all will be well in the
end, for the form will rise in
the figure of a revelation: a
startling desire transformed into
a mystical symbol. here is the
sign you had always sought,

not the absolute so much
as the relative in pursuit
of the absolute. follow this
sign into that other world,
and you will make of art something
real, a poem of transport
and of the heart of life as well—

a daring prophecy to the
future of the substance of
your own life: before its
serpent wakes and smothers it,
lashes it up and out into the
boundless ether, the nonrepentent,
nonreproductive void.

EPILOGUE

THE TRANSCENDENCE OF APOLLO

across the sky, above
the continental bridge,
a cloud moved with such
fury and velocity
all eyes were captivated.
it was as if the day
had fallen unnaturally to

the night and the dark
had achieved its magic
of despair. the crowd thronged
unto the precipice to observe:
what would happen to
the melancholy they felt
if it were unloosened into

the cloud, now racing
toward them with immaculate
speed? what hand could
stop their fear, or the cloud
from its appointed disgrace?
how many lives would it take
to say no, we are free of the

portents? it was September
and the cloud disturbed
the quiet death of summer.
it was that unblemished
feeling of renewal all held
as the favored children
of the sun—not simply

the bronze adventure
in the waves, or the
love making of the young
on the midnight shore, but
the turbulent depths of heat
and radiance playing the
music of a scandalous

violin. it was that kind
of sun in which the light
trickles into an innermost
pool, and yet in its silence
inspires a voluptuous music,
sustained into the darkening days.
(O cloud, you are the demon

we had hoped would never
return). . . . and so the rains
fell upon their perplexity—
and wet they stood, and
naked, before the music.
and suddenly it took on
the throbs of a spasm—

a choleric fever they
wished forever dead.
the bridge began to sway
in the distance; or was it
a mirage, now startled
by that confabulation they
had carried on their historical

backs? the rains drilled
them with mechanical
disgust, and they began to
scream at one another above
the din. the cloud roared
its pleasure, a fantasy on the
metaphysical order, to come

true. what dreams they spoke
of in ascent became barbarous
chants, a disorder of a
magnitude to cheat the skies.
now monadic, they rolled their eyes
as if seeking the solitude of death—
and stroked the music silent. . . .

in a certain sense, there
was beauty in the storm
as it unfolded before them:
how easily the azure had
given way to the dark phantom
that swallowed every particle
of light, a dragon whose

tongue swept up the blue
and burst into flame
at the same time. it was
a theater now whose lights
suddenly dampened for
the change of scene, the
massive exodus of day

and all the participants
of life—for the heath
and the metaphysical dark.
it was unavoidable violence,
a cosmic transformation
to show the lingerers of
destiny another knowledge . . .

rip and spit, rip and spit,
thunder and the miraculous
flashes of the dragon's
jaws. for this is the sublime
when it enters the conditions
of life, a strangeness,
a foreign terror whose

very otherness charges
the eyes of the mundane.
they held themselves together
by the bar of the dragon's
flash, the blue fire now
enveloping them in their joy;
they danced with rapacious

passion. the music became
overwhelmingly loud, rocking
them to their soul-center,
reverberating as the absence
of an idea. . . . for this time
they lost the terror of
the cloud—though it too

loomed with the intensity
of a volcano. each danced
within a solitude out of
the inner music, while the
collective beat caught them
in its frenzy. the cloud
coughed and the earth

began to flood. what
had happened to perception
now that their eyes had
turned inward? can frenetic
hearts ever attain that knowledge
held as the bursting of
the cosmos? someone must

orchestrate the music before
the world ends in exhaustion,
someone must give order
to the deep pain, so that
it will not dissipate as
mere excess. the dancers
suddenly began to pull

their hair out, while the sky
darkened between the dragon's
deafening flashes—but no one was
left to see the bridge falling into
the stark waters, pitch black
with tiger waves; no one was
left to see the steel dynamo

vanish . . .
except one, who had been
observing the observers at
the rear of the stage near
the wings. he was painting
the scene with words, attempting
to find in all the turmoil

an image—not simply
descriptive but dynamic—
of the rage, what could
potentially contain the terror
in a frozen metaphor, a
plastic form to endure
the floods overarching

the perishing land. he had
hoped to construct a language
of the discord—a language,
that is, to make the world still
before silence was forever
smothered. this was a challenge
to all the tendons of thought,

for he had never witnessed
such an extreme catastrophe,
like bowels being ripped from
human and world in one
breath, remarkable
he held his ground. . . .
it was a delicate art he had

inherited—to possess the
music in ways it would
not possess, to sustain
the spirit without the frenzy.
it was a passion he must
capture short of ecstasy—
love at the threshold of death.

he called on all the powers
of his craft, like an
athlete seeking mastery
over his body. it was that
words could not be held
down in the flood tide,
it was the bridge cracking

against internal rhythms.
his solitude, he surmised,
was more profound than ever
before—and all was
conspiring against his art.
the cloud gave off its
cacaphony and the crowd

spoke to it with hands
waving, pounding their chests.
in the theater of nature,
order can never be assumed,
and he knew this with
the inner knowledge of an
ancient scribe. but he could

not hesitate, for he
could see in the future
how this scene would all
deconstruct. that was the
worst of his trial—for his
foresight demanded expostulation. . . .
what tears there would be

when the flood waters
leapt upon the earth, what
rancor and self-mutilation,
what rupturing of the two
continents, whose destiny
once met in infinity.
and the world would be

finished not as fact
so much, but as form.
it was with this knowledge
that he himself broke down,
weeping into the rising flood.
what could ease him of the
pain of prophecy, what could

alleviate that burden of
ancient consciousness
made sharper by this crisis?
his weeping intensified,
a nostalgic longing for
the ancestral past when
the music was never so vexing,

and order never so
evasive. it was the weeping
that brought him to an
almost suicidal leap: because
the past and the future seemed
annulled in the pulse of an instant,
in the whisper of a nightingale

on the brooding stage.
but it was the weeping also
that freed him for the act,
a releasing of the turmoil
he had for so long confined.
he could kiss the universe again;
it was as if a poem had also

been freed in the overflow
of tears; it was as if a
language had once more crept
upon the stage. it was at the
point before the sea had passed
over the earth, when the clamor
became the crush of a human

stampede; it was at the
point just before the cloud
and crowd had conspired
to draw a close to the tragic
drama; at that point when
fear and terror gave way to
surrender, to the unconscious

wave—a wave that would
roll all memory away;
it was at this point he once
more discovered the heroic,
and with his painted words
awoke the sleeping image:
a love constructed out of

language, a love to stir
the music and to quell.
for it was music he rescued
from the lost shore, devoid
of the fanatic, a music of
clear notes, bright and green.
here was the image,

a frozen nightingale singing
its depths of silence. here
was the stillness he had
labored for. a book forever
closed whose meanings will
never die. such is the scene
swept of mendacity, such

the tragic clarity he sought
in the nightingale's song.
where was the next challenge,
where were those wings to take
him beyond gratitude? here was
the nightingale—enough to
imagine its flight; for he had

envisioned these wings on so
many occasions in the past,
with little hope of their ever
soaring—like the hawk of his
memory at the transom of death.
now he was free of his labors,
free for the moment to meditate.

he had come so close to the end,
all he could think of was rest, rest on
the promontory beyond the scene.
above the world, in the stillness of
perpetual motion, he would sit, sit,
and gaze upon the ocean of two spheres . . .
he would rest but never die.